GOD'S REVELATION OF MY GENESIS

MY GENESIS

Kim Lue

Publisher: Luminous Publishing
www.luminouspublishing.com
For bulk orders or other inquiries, email:
info@luminouspublishing.com

What did I do to cause so much pleasure for other people? What is it about me that welcomed offenders to take me against my will?

— Kim Lue

DEDICATION

To: God the Father, God the Son and God the Holy Spirit

This book would not have been possible without all Your instructions. You have been a mighty force in me to write this book. I am in awe of what You have accomplished in me and through me. I am so glad that You are Omnipresent—You are always with me everywhere I go. You are Omnipotent—You have all power in Your hands, and whatever is in Your hands, no man can take it out, and whatever You pluck out of Your hands, no man can put back in. You are Omniscient—You know everything.

Lord, I will always remember what You told me over ten years ago, that Jesus is in front of me, leading the way. Your grace and mercy are behind me, following me all the days of my life. My Guardian Angels, your hedge of protection is on the left and right side of me, keeping me safe from any hurt, harm, and danger that may come upon me, and You (God) are up above and looking down upon me. How can I lose with the stuff You use? My answer is, I CAN'T.

TABLE OF CONTENTS

PROLOGUE

To all my Sisters and Brothers in Christ (Ministers), I know it has been hard on many of us in our walk with Christ. Yet, if we don't grow weary in well-doing, if we faint not, and if we continue to walk the walk of faith and run the race as the Holy Spirit leads us, we will see the promises of God, and we will see it in the land of the living. Just as we suffer with Christ, we will reign with Christ and receive our due reward in the end, which is eternal life.

So, I say stay PRAYERFUL, keep FASTING, and keep BELIEVING and TRUSTING in GOD because we can't make it without Him. We can do all things through Christ that gives us the strength. We must not be complacent in our work for God. We must start from the beginning (Genesis) of our lives to see where it all started and then walk out of our Genesis into our Exodus (exit). Only then can our sins and slavery be left behind.

Our Leviticus awaits us. It is waiting to teach us how to be holy and worship the true and living God. As we go forward into our Numbers, we will find that there are stumbling blocks called whining, disobedience, murmuring, complaining and discontentment waiting for us to hinder our journey into our promise land. But we must remember our Deuteronomy because it reminds us of where we come from and how we got there; it reminds us of who God is and what God has already done for us in this walk with Him.

As we travel on through our wilderness experiences, we must remember the Joshuas of our time, who have helped lead and guide us on some of our journeys. The Joshuas, who were obedient to God, taught us how to fight the enemy and follow our basic instructions before leaving earth. We need these instructions daily because eventually, we will come upon the Judges who will judge us for our sins. Still, we must remember one thing as Ministers: God forgives us for our sins and there is restoration for those who have a relationship with Him and those who will repent.

So, we must be careful that our sins don't control and overtake us, and maybe, just maybe, the Judges will be lenient in our cause. We must be a Ruth at all times: strong in character and faithful to God, even when society around us is collapsing. Be steadfast, unmovable, and unstoppable. We must remember Ruth's famous words:

"Don't ask me to leave you and turn back, wherever you go, I will go. Wherever you live, I will live. Your people will be my people, and your God will be my God."

- Ruth 1:16

With this remark, I want to say to my Sisters and Brothers in Christ that we are the Ruths of this generation and we must remain as one in Christ, be there for one another, lifting each other when one of us is down. As the song says, 'I need you, and you need me because we are a part of God's Body' (I Need You to Survive by Hezekiah Walker). Stand with me (like Ruth), agree with me; it is God's will that we supply each other's needs, so we each can survive. We realize that people will try to make us stumble and fall and get us sidetracked in our walk with Christ. Just tell them, "I Am Ruth."

We must also have some Samuel in us. Helpful, full of wisdom, giving people messages from God, keeping our heart pure before God, and making a difference in the Kingdom of God. As we read the first three chapters in the book of Kings, remember that we have to be like David. To follow God with integrity and godliness and obey all God's commands, decrees and regulations. Even if we stumble and fall, we must get back up, repent, dust off our shoes and continue to go forward.

We must be men and women after God's own heart. Then be like Elijah in the book of Kings, a great prophet and stand for God, stand with God, because you plus God are the majority, and if God is on our side, it's a win-win situation. Remember, if God is for you, who can be against you, what can man do to you? They can kill your physical body, but they can't touch your soul.

I could go on and on into all 66 books of the Bible and show who we should model after. All of us fit somewhere in the books of the Bible. We must know who we are and whose we are; that's half the battle.

INTRODUCTION

Now I Understand

In the 1st chapter of Jeremiah, God said He knew me before I was in my mother's womb. He knew me before I was ever born because He sanctified me. I always wondered what I looked like at the beginning of my life before I came to the earth realm, when I was still in heaven as a spirit, living with my Father, GOD. I often ponder about things like: did I have flesh in heaven? Did I have hair, fingernails, eyes, ears, a nose? Or was I a spirit? Did other spirits and I recognize one another? Did I have friends in heaven? What kind of games did we play? Is there a playground in heaven with merry-go-rounds, see-saws, and swings? What do spirits in heaven like to do? Do they have jobs or things to keep them busy? Or do we always praise and worship the Lord? Were we being taught about the earthly realm before we got here, or were we taught heavenly things only? Did we know about our assignments for the earth while we were still in heaven? Are there grownups in heaven? Or are the Father, Son, and the Holy Spirit the only adults? What about children? Were we perfect little spirits, or were we mischievous, like most worldly kids? Did we get spankings? Or were we always pure—not knowing good and evil at that time.

These are some of the questions I asked God but haven't gotten all the answers yet. I feel like God will answer them in His own time. Timing is everything. Plus, God knows what is, and some things are better off unknown. People often say that you don't question God, but how will you ever know the truth if you don't? My Bible says in the book of Matthew 7:7, *"Ask and it will be given to you; seek, and you will find; knock, and the door will be opened unto you."* Does your Bible not say the same? Believe me, I have been knocking on heaven's door a long time, and the door to my heart is now open because I'm seeking to hear a word from the Lord. They also say that curiosity kills the cat. Boy! I'm glad I'm not a cat.

Many years ago, God spoke heaven and earth into existence. He separated the light from darkness and commanded the waters of heaven and earth to separate. He commanded the dry ground to produce a mist and water the land, which brought forth the seed-bearing fruits and plants. Then God marked the days, seasons, and years, and positioned the stars, sun, and the moon in the sky to govern the night. Before I was in my mother's womb, He set me apart for the assignment He planned for me. Jeremiah 29:11 says, *"For I know the plans I have for you,"* says the LORD. *"They are plans for good and not for disaster, to give you a future and a hope."*

That's when it happened. Somewhere in all this calculation of time, the Almighty Creator, also known as YAHWEH (God), thought about little me; I was now part of the Genesis 1:26 movement.

I believe this means I was a spirit first before I was flesh, just like Jesus. He was a spirit first, except Jesus came miraculously in the flesh by the Holy Spirit of God through a woman, keeping Him pure and holy, without sin, to save us. Let's talk about our salvation a little bit before we go any farther. I heard a conversation in heaven between God, the Father, and His Son Jesus. I imagined God saying He needed to find someone to go down to earth to save His people. Jesus said, "Father, I'll go." The Father said, "Son, you don't understand, they are going to beat you, whip you, spit on you, pierce you in the side, and make a mockery of you to your death." Jesus says, "I don't care. Father, I still want to go."

Still, the Father says, "Son, you don't understand that they are going to take you from judgment hall to judgment hall trying to persecute you." However, Jesus said, "I still want to go, Father." But the Father said, "Son, you still don't understand that after it's all said and done, they will unjustly accuse you, crucify you, and put you in a borrowed tomb." Jesus says, "That's okay, Father. Send me; I'll go." He said, "Father, there's one thing good about putting me in a borrowed tomb...anything borrowed must be given back to its rightful owner.

Considering that the tomb belongs to a rich man, tells me they must bury me with the rich, and I will rise richer than before my crucifixion." Then Jesus said, "Father, there is one more thing I see in my future, and that is that borrowed tomb will not be able to hold me. I will RISE and return home to you. Father, please let me go, send me, Father." So, the Father replies to Jesus, "Okay, Son, you can go, but remember this one thing...I'll never leave you nor forsake you. I will always be with you."

Romans 5:8 says, *"But God demonstrates His love for us in this: While we were still sinners, Christ died for us."* Even though He knew He would be wounded for our transgressions and bruised for our iniquities, Jesus was still willing to die for the sins of the world. He knew all the hurt and pain He was going to endure, but it did not stop Him from wanting to come to earth to save us. So, God takes a piece of Himself (which is Jesus) and gives it to the Holy Spirit, and the Holy Spirit implants Jesus in the womb of Mary, a virgin.

On the way to the cross, Jesus carried all our sins with Him. Our sins were like a garment; they covered Him from head to toe. Our sins tried to overtake Him, but it couldn't because Jesus knew His assignment and was determined to complete it to the end. Thank God He did. The Bible says in Psalm 34:19, *"Many are the afflictions of the righteous, But the LORD delivers him out of them all."* This tells me every man or woman, boy or girl has or will have sins (afflictions) in this lifetime, and Jesus bore them. Including the people who have not been born yet. What an awesome God.

Our sins weighed Jesus down more than the cross did. Picture Jesus crucified at Golgotha for the sins of rape, murder, stealing, homosexuality, backbiting, slander, adultery, fornication, condemnation, lies, false accusations, impurities, lust, hostility, quarreling, jealousy, anger, selfish ambition, dissension, arrogance, envy, idolatry, sorcery, drunkenness, wild parties, cheating, greed and more. All these sins in the form and shape of a cross. The sins of the world tried to kill Jesus, but they could not. Jesus laid down His life. Why? So that death wouldn't have any power over Him or us, Hallelujah!

Our sins were overwhelming; that's why Jesus asked the Father to take the bitter cup from Him, but God's grace was sufficient. Sin is a killer, and you can die and go straight to hell in your sin for all eternity. Why did Jesus die for us? So, we could have a relationship again with God, the Father. Because God turned His back on humanity, He closed His ears and eyes to mankind, and worse of all, He shut off His voice from us.

Mankind was lost; they had no choice but to go to hell because God hated their sins. Sin back then and today's sins are plentiful and still running rampant. There is nothing new under the sun. God was grieved that He ever made man. (Genesis 6:6) God did not like what mankind became, but He did love us unconditionally. Before Jesus came to save us, Satan had the freedom to make us sin as much as we would allow him to, because we didn't always know that we had the authority to trample on snakes and scorpions. We didn't know we had power over the enemy's weapons.

Without hearing God's voice, you will go astray, just like a lost sheep. People are just like sheep, and all sheep need a shepherd to guide them on their straight and narrow path. Hello, somebody! I am talking to you and me! All sheep (us) need to know our Shepherd's (God's) voice.

Jesus loves us unconditionally, despite our sin and flaws. When we nailed Jesus' hands to the cross, we thought we were taking all His power away, but it just made Him even more powerful. According to Habakkuk 3:4, when God's HAND is mentioned in the Bible, it is referencing His POWER. When we nailed His feet to the cross, we thought we could keep Him from going forward, we thought we could make Him come down off that cross and give up on saving us. But Jesus said, "No! Not so." We were those "crooked nails" that hung Jesus on the cross.

I thank God that He knows how to straighten out crooked nails (us). When we crowned His head with thorns and started calling Him "Jesus the King of the Jews," we thought we were making a mockery of Him, but we were making a fool out of ourselves because He was the King of the Jews as well as the Gentiles. And like every KING, He deserved a CROWN.

We thought that crowning Jesus with those thorns would mess up His mind, but it didn't. He was tormented in His body, but He never lost His mind. He was pierced in His side, but He never lost

His mind. His hands and feet were nailed to the cross, but He never lost His mind. We are worthy, valuable, and belong to Jesus because He bought us with a price. His blood was our ransom. Whatever we must go through, Jesus paid the price for it on Calvary. He died for the saints and the sinners. His death gave us a more abundant life for all eternity with Him and the Father.

Jesus did not only pray in the Garden of Gethsemane for the disciples. Jesus prayed for you and me in the Garden of Gethsemane; that God would help keep His mind stable. If it weren't for Jesus, we wouldn't have an abundant life. We wouldn't have a choice to be good or bad; we would have remained a crooked nail. We wouldn't have an option to be holy or unholy; we would have stayed a crooked nail. The devil would have free access to rule, reign, and abide in us.

This world and the people as we know it now would be messed up even more if Jesus hadn't died and resurrected. If Jesus had lost His mind during the crucifixion, it would have meant His coming would have been in vain. But thank God He didn't lose His mind. Hallelujah! Jesus is the one who paved the way for you and me. It was not Prophet Mohammed, it was not Buddha, and it was not Lucifer who is better known as Satan. What an awesome God we serve!

In the beginning, God's word tells me that I was born in sin and shaped in iniquity. How could this be? I had not learned to scoot, crawl, or even walk yet. I just got here, God! What could I have done as a baby to deserve a prize such as SIN? My first father and mother, Adam and Eve, were deceived by the snake in the garden. That upset God, and He put them out of the garden.

When I was born, I became accountable for their mistakes, the product of a generational curse from the very beginning. Just like I had no say in who my birth mother and father were, I didn't have a say about whether or not I wanted to enter into sin. Now isn't that something? Now, I realize that I have a choice of whether I want to sin or not. We all must have a made-up mind whether we want to be sinners or saints in this life. Whatever our choices are, we will be held accountable for them.

Now I know it will all work out in Revelation (The End). I didn't understand how years ago, people would say, "You can't see it, you're blind." I would say to myself, what could they possibly mean? Are these people crazy? I see just fine! I see the beautiful trees and the blue seas, the different types of birds, the dogs, cats and the people. I now understand I wasn't seeing. Yes, I saw the physical things but not the spiritual.

I understand it now, that I can see in the different realms of the spirit world. How different it is from anything. I used to think that I was better off not knowing certain things; the less I knew, the better off I was. Now I know that isn't true. Not knowing could be hazardous to your health. It could kill you and take you out when you are not aware of your spiritual surroundings. It's like being served a meal you've never had before made by someone you don't know or trust. The unknown can be scary sometimes.

For example, when someone joins your church and you hear some things about him or her that doesn't sit well with you, does this make you leery about eating what they are cooking? I used to be that person. I now know that whatever the enemy tries to do to me, whatever he tries to poison me with, whatever trap he sets against me, won't prosper.

Warning always comes before destruction. You can get warnings in your prayer and study time with God, during your meditation, and in your fasting time with God. You must know God's voice. If God is your Shepherd, you should know His voice. Familiar spirits will come to you as if they were God if you aren't discerning. They try to imitate Him. Beware of false gods that come as angels of light. The devil is the father of all lies, and the truth is not in him. You need to get to know God for yourself and have a relationship with Him.

You need to know the Word of God too. Read the Bible and eat the whole loaf from Genesis to Revelation because if you eat bits and pieces of it, you may miss out on the main ingredients. I love the acronym used for the word, *Bible* which stands for "Basic Instructions Before Leaving Earth." The Bible gives us the road map to our daily lives, and if you understand it, you will be led by the Spirit of God in the direction you must go.

Please be mindful that it is not always an easy road because the enemy comes on our path to distract us, to kill, steal, and destroy us (John 10:10). Be aware of the enemy's tactics and know that the battle with the enemy starts in the mind. I was placed on this earth to fight for a victory that Jesus Christ already won. The fight was fixed from the very beginning of time. The battle was won years ago on Calvary. Still, we are to read and study to show ourselves approved, and we must fight, watch, and always pray in the Holy Spirit.

When I am studying or reading, I remind myself that God's Word (The Bible) is an asset to me. It is my bread of life; it is my lifeline. It is my CPR (Cardiac, Pulmonary, respiration). Why? Because it resurrects me from all the dead things in my life that mean me no good. The drugs, alcohol, stealing, fornication, all the wiles of the enemy. The Bible is your Bread of Life, and you must eat the whole loaf. From Genesis to Revelation. Don't leave a crumb wasted. Read it line upon line, precept upon precept. If you read the entire Bible with understanding, you will be made whole.

Each slice of bread you eat (the page you read) gives you daily nutrition. One page may have healing Scriptures in it. One may have deliverance. You may need hope, comfort, peace, victory, or need to feel loved. Where is a better place to get all the things you need than in God's love letter? God's love letter written to us through men who were inspired by the Holy Spirit. God's love letter teaches us how to walk in our valley lows, humble ourselves on our mountain tops, have self-discipline, and apply His Word to our everyday lives. The whole loaf has Jesus' blood and love flowing through it, and it teaches us from beginning to end (Genesis to Revelation) how to run this race to the end. So, I say once again, eat your wonder bread, eat your bread of life, eat the whole loaf, read the entire Bible with understanding, and we will endure to the end.

CHAPTER ONE

My Genesis

I was born to Oletha and Edward on November 19, 1956, in Mexico, Missouri. We lived in a little gray house on Holt Street. I suppose I was just fine being the only child for two years, and then she came, my little sister. When she came on the scene, I stayed in trouble all the time because I was more of a follower back then than a leader. I was what you would call a daredevil, and I would try just about anything if I thought I could get away with it. I thought I was just a typical kid doing typical kid things.

It was a scorching summer day in 1963 when my great-grandmother was on the porch just swinging and smoking what used to be a viceroy cigarette dangling from her mouth. All you could see was the filter in her mouth with ashes still hanging on. I never understood how she did that magic trick with the ashes never falling from the butt of the cigarette.

It was 100 degrees or more on this day, and my sister and I were out playing when my grandmother called for me. She wanted me to get her a drink of water. Three times she called me. I began to feel like a Hebrew slave fetching for the master because it was always, "Kim do this, Kim do that," I was ready to change my name, and if she didn't guess what it was, I wouldn't have to answer her, because my grandmother wore me and my name out every day. She never called my sister's name one time if I was there. The only time they ever called on my sister was when she was being rewarded with some treat.

After calling my name for the fourth time on this day was a charm. I was tired of her calling me to do her dirty work. The little princess never had to do anything for her, only little ol' me. Out of nowhere, my sister asked me if I wanted to pay my grandmother back for worrying me all the time. Of course, I said yes, it sounded good to me. So, my sister tells me to give her some water out of the toilet stool, that would fix her. So, I said yes, but I wanted to be nice about it. So, I flushed the toilet first and then gave her a clean tin cup of cool water. My grandmother told me that it was the best water she ever had, so she sent me to fetch her the 2nd cup, and I gave it to her.

As the day went by, my mother came home, and my sister told my mom what I had done, and I got whipped and punished for it. I should've said the devil made me do it (As Flip Wilson would say). Isn't that just like the devil to suggest something to you, and then you get in trouble for it? But I have to remember one thing: I had a choice, and I chose to follow the devil.

We must remember that Satan has no power over us except what we allow for him to have and what little power God the Father gave him. In the book of Luke 10:19, it says, *"We have the authority in Christ Jesus to trample over snakes and scorpions, and over all power of the enemy…"* Or should I say we have authority over the people who allow Satan to use them unknowingly! *"…nothing shall by any means hurt us."*

I have learned that the best way to trample over the snakes, scorpions, or people is with the Word of God! We can't bring a gun or knife to this fight because it will only kill the flesh and not the spirit. We must know that there are always two entities (spirits) working. It's either the Holy Ghost or the hella ghost. The hella ghost led me. The hella ghost is the devil's spirit, and the Holy Ghost is God's Spirit.

When someone passes away (the flesh is what dies), the spirit is still alive and well. You must know that spirits are real, and they are not all here to be friends with you, but they will befriend you to get all the information they need to use against you. Another way to keep Satan from using us is to keep our mouths shut. Sometimes we talk a little too much, giving the enemy too much information to work with, and this is what he uses against us—our mouths!

My little sister caused me to get in quite a bit of trouble throughout my childhood. She was always mischievous when adults weren't around, and she always wanted to do something

18

she knew was wrong but didn't want to do the wrong thing by herself. She grew up a lot quicker than I did and became my boss, second to my mom. I will never forget this toilet water episode as long as I live. I will take it with me to my grave. If only I knew then what I know now. I have had my share of learning experiences, and some of the lessons I am just learning because of my lack of knowledge as a child.

The Bible says in Proverbs 22:6, *"Train up a child in the way he should go: and when he is old, he will not depart from it."* The Holy Spirit will bring everything taught back to their remembrance. So, teach them God's way because God's way is the only correct way. I'm glad that I sent my three children to church to learn about God the Father, our Savior Jesus Christ, and the Holy Ghost. Some of them are doing their own thing now, but I believe what the Word says; they will come back to God. I pray daily for God to draw them nigh unto Him. Trust me that God knows what's best for our children and us. You must be obedient to what God tells you through His Spirit that lives in you. *"He who has an ear let him hear what the spirit of the Lord is saying."* (Revelation 2:11)

Here we are in the latter year of 1963, living in the projects on Christy Street, well, to my amazement, all hell is starting to break loose. I minded my own business, leaving everybody else's alone when along comes my sister throwing out her bait to reel me in, and of course, I take the bait, hook, line, and sinker. "Come on, come on," she says, "I want to show you something." We go up to the bathroom, and she pulls out this Viceroy cigarette (the same kind my grandmother was smoking on the porch). She starts to smoke it, blowing it out of the bathroom window. She then gives it to me. I begin to smoke it and blow it out the window as well, when all of a sudden, I hear my mom's voice, "Kim, is that you blowing smoke out that window?" Caught once again. "Come downstairs right now!" I go, scared and worried at the same time. I wanted to beat my sister up once and for all, but this wasn't the time. NO! NOT YET. Well, I get another whipping and got put on punishment again. I couldn't go outside and play with my friends, but she did.

All I remember hearing was Kim, you are the oldest, and you should be setting an example for your sister and brothers. My thought was, *why didn't you punish her too? She was the one with the great influence and ideas.* Sometime later, my sister and I jumped up and down on the bed, which was against the rules, and I jumped so high I hit the light fixture coming from the ceiling and split my head open. Blood was gushing out.

My sister called for my mom, and she came running upstairs to see what was going on with me. She took one look at me and said, "You need stitches, but I am not taking you to the hospital because I have told you over and over again about jumping up and down in the bed." I don't remember how long it took to get me to the hospital, but I didn't go to the hospital until my stepdad came home from work.

Some days later, while upstairs playing in my room, voices from downstairs were calling to my sister and me, "come down here, there is someone here to see you!" Low and behold, the Welfare Office (DFS) came to move us out of our home. We cried and cried, shouting, "please don't take us away, we will be good! We will start minding our mom and grandmother! Please give us another chance! We won't be bad anymore!"

Truthfully, I didn't realize we were all that bad or naughty. I thought my sister should have gone because she was the instigator of all the things we did wrong. This pleading went on for 20 or 30 minutes, and finally, the agent said, "We are going to put you in a really nice home with other foster children and foster parents." We most definitely were not trying to hear what this man was saying. We were trying to convince our mom to give us a second chance. We apologized repeatedly, and finally, it worked. We got another chance, so we thought. But later, we found out that the agent was not a welfare agent or foster care agent at all. He was just an insurance agent coming to collect his money and to SCARE US STRAIGHT! It worked for a little while!

After everything Jesus has done to make life better for me, I found myself as a young girl on the earth, here in the flesh, with absolutely no experience in how to live on earth, not knowing what to expect out of the world or the people in it. What am I doing here on earth? What is in it for me? What is this thing called LIFE all about? What is my destiny? Thank God He is omnipresent and with me all the time, even though at the time I didn't realize it. Thank God He is omnipotent and knows me better than anyone, including myself. He knew what I would look like, how tall and big I would be, and how He would turn my life upside down without my permission. Thank God He is omniscient and has all power in His hands to control me and my sinful nature.

I needed the desire to be maintained and kept, I had to know I needed a Savior, and now I do. Thank God He clothed me when I was naked, meaning He took care of me even when I didn't have a relationship with Him. I was naked because I was full of sin; I wasn't cleaned yet. I was naked because I was full of unrighteousness and unholiness—making me the walking dead because the Holy Spirit wasn't leading me.

When I finally found Jesus, He clothed my nakedness. He took my nakedness of unrighteousness and clothed me with righteousness. He took my unholiness and clothed me with holiness. He took my stinking thinking and dressed me in my right mind. He took my sin and clothed me with purification. His blood washed me and made me whiter than snow. Now the Holy Spirit lives in me.

CHAPTER 2

Why Me?

It was 1964, and I was only eight years old when this black, cute, perfect-toothed guy came along. Let's call him THE NEIGHBOR. I would see him walking by our apartment every day just smiling and winking at me. He was 15 or 16 years old. I didn't realize that this boy was checking me out at the time, watching my every move. I'm sure he was contemplating in his mind the right time and place for him to make his move on me. It gives me chills up and down my spine as I think more and more about this offender because when I look back at the situation, the offender had a dark faraway look about him, as most offenders do.

On this particular night, it happened. THE NEIGHBOR raped me in our backyard; blood was everywhere. In my panties, running down my legs, on my fingertips, and there was pain in my stomach. I was scared; I mean terrified. Scared to go into my own house. I trembled with fear and grief because I believed it was my fault. I must have done something for this to happen to me.

I couldn't figure out for the life of me what it was. I was afraid to tell anyone because he said if I did, he would do it again, and he told me that it was my fault and that my mom would not believe me. He said she would blame me for what happened. I kept hearing his voice over and over again in my mind saying, "Don't tell no one because it's your fault." The devil had me where he wanted me, scared, scarred, and upset.

I was terrified to say anything, and I didn't want anybody in my family to see me, so I went quietly into the house. My mom was gone, and my grandmother was nowhere in sight. Pain! Pain! Pain! That is all I felt. I tried holding my stomach in one place, not wanting to upset it worse. I ran my bathwater, hopped into the tub, and just sat there, crying and sobbing, wondering if it would get back to my mom.

I did everything I could to keep her from finding out. I wrapped the bloody underwear in a brown paper sack and put it in the very bottom of the trash can outside so that if anyone opened the lid, they wouldn't notice it. After that day, I was so afraid of THE NEIGHBOR.

He was now a big black monster to me, and after that, all monsters looked like him. My childhood was not the same; I stayed terrified and afraid of certain men who looked like him. I judged all dark-skinned black men as monsters for a long time. This rape became one of many hidden traumatic events I buried deep inside the soul of my fragile body. It took days, months, even years to get it out of my mind.

I was brought up in the church as a little kid, which helped to set the foundation of my faith. I heard about Jesus, but I didn't get saved until I was in my twenties. A friend of mine who was a Christian preacher inspired me to have a relationship with Jesus. One thing I have learned in my many years of hurts and pains is that God kept me. It was nothing I did; it was my Creator who held me and consoled me. No one else knew about the hurt and pain I had gone through but God. Since He created me, I now see that He was the only one who knew how to put my broken pieces back together again.

In May of 1965, we moved away from Christy Street, away from those memories of rape, pain, and agony, but little did I know, the hidden trauma moved with me too. We were living on a new street called Bolivar Street; I was safe. There was nothing for me to worry about, no one to harm me; I was free. But what I didn't know was that same devilish spirit was in this neighborhood too. That same spirit of rape in THE NEIGHBOR was also living in someone else as my new neighbor.

Five years later, in 1970, my mom sent me to our neighbor's house to get my sister. I was around 14 years old when it happened again. He was a black, tall, scary-looking guy. We will call him THE BLACK KNIGHT. He calls me over to him, supposedly to tell me something. I wasn't expecting him to rape me in our backyard, but he did right next to the fence. It was a little blood this time, but a lot of pain, and boy was I afraid. He became the devil to me. He told me not to tell anybody and that it was his word against mine. I told somebody, my friend, and she promised not to tell anyone. She didn't; she took it to her grave. Now, I wish she were in the land of the living to verify what I told her, but God knows I'm telling the truth, and that devil knows it too.

Of course, I thought this incident was my fault once again. I remember it well. It was like a cold winter's night when he pulled me close to him and wrapped his body tight around me like a coat. "I BEEN WATCHING YOU, AND I WANT YOU," he growled. I tried to get away, but I failed. I laid there, numb in the image of death, hurt and angry, asking God to help me. I would ask myself, is there a God? Does He love me, as the song says? *Jesus loves me this, I know.* I felt like I was going to die.

As time went on, I tried to forget all my hurt, hate, and pain toward the black knight. I tried to hold on and not drive myself crazy. Thank God, I finally became at peace with myself. Still, this rape became another hidden trauma too. Now I was carrying two weights. Both were suppressed from my memory because I wanted to forget. I couldn't understand for the life of me why God would let these things happen to me. I was a church-going girl; I went to church every time the church doors opened. But I guess if these things had to happen to someone, why not me?

Maybe someone else couldn't live through these things I did. I started writing poems a few years later about different stuff, and I wrote the following poem for this incident.

THE BLACK KNIGHT

Like a coat that needed to be fastened to keep out the wind,
all my troubles have started again.

He pulled me closer and closer to him saying,
"I've been watching you and I want you, Kim."

I tried to fight but I didn't succeed—
all I could feel was his selfish greed.

Now the Black Knight has raped me too,
I'm scared, hurt, and alone with nothing to do.

He had been watching me both day and night,
and he got me when the time was right.

Was I just an open market, for the enemy to use
and choose to hit a bull's-eye in this target?

I feel like I want to run, run, run, I am blaming myself
for what The Black Night had done.

Right now, I'm feeling so ashamed,
because I thought I was to blame.

Oh, how I wish that I was dead,
with all these terrible memories dancing in my head.

With no one to talk to and with no one to trust,
It was just me and my broken heart that was truly crushed.

As the days, weeks, months, and years went by, I forced myself to remember the trauma no more. The memories laid dormant compacted deep within my soul, just waiting for the right time to explode. The guilt and shame haunted me later in life to the point where it felt like a losing battle. Scripture reminds us in 2 Chronicles 20:15 not be discouraged by the struggle. Do not be afraid of them or discouraged because of the vast army of offenders and child molesters. Why? Because God will take care of those, who harm you.

You see, when they touched me, they touched God. The Word says in Psalm 105:15, *"Touch not my anointed and do my prophets (Prophetess) no harm."* Those who do you harm, and even those who harmed me, are held accountable for what they did. Even though I didn't know I was called, anointed, and a prophetess at the time of my loss, God knew. The Bible says in the book of Ephesians 1:11 that God chose us in advance, He appointed us, and He makes everything work out according to His plan. Even though I didn't answer the call on my life at a young age, the fact remains that God called me in advance, before I was ever born, and God knew that I would answer the call in His timing and not my own.

Now I know that when those who offended me many years ago touched me, they touched the HEART OF GOD. They will have to battle with God and not me. You and I are gifts from God to our mothers, fathers, and others. When you receive a gift, you handle it gently with care, not wanting to break what is inside of it. Yet some people will not handle you gently. They will toss and turn you, flip, tangle, and even ripped open your neat package in a hurry, not worrying about how fragile the GIFT is inside.

In my case, they wanted to get to the gift that was supposed to be meant for my husband. It's good to know that this battle is not mine but the Lord's. 2 Chronicles 20:17 says, *"You will not have to fight this battle, take up your positions, stand firm, and see the deliverance the LORD will give you. Go out, face your enemy tomorrow, and the LORD will be with you."* God knows where it hurts them the most, better than you do. I realized that if I try to fight my way, I may hurt myself because God might whip them and me for getting in His way.

Remember, God doesn't need our help to do His job. We need His. I'm glad that I can face them without fear because God didn't give me the spirit of fear, but a spirit of power, love, and a sound mind. I can treat them kind, smile, and feed them with a long handle spoon. I hate what they did to me, and God does too. The Bible says that we must love those who despitefully use us if we want to get into heaven, but that doesn't mean you have to like them.

In our house on Bolivar Street, I would have dreams and visions of this red devil with a pitchfork that would come on the wall for me to see. I remember three times staring at the devil on the wall, paralyzed with fear. How frightening it was to lay an inch away from my sister in bed and not be able to reach or talk to her. I couldn't wake her up to help me and for her to see what I saw. All I could do was pray for God to help me.

Months later, I saw the image of a devil again on the same wall. It was a warning sign for me, but at the time, I didn't know it was a warning. I just knew I was scared of it and how it made me feel. Seeing these images went on from the time I was 12 years of age until I was 14 years old. I had no one to talk to about what was going on.

I wish I'd known the scriptures back then. I didn't know that God gave me the authority to trample on snakes and scorpions and over all the power of the enemy and that nothing shall by any means hurt me (Luke 10:19). This means that whatever the enemy uses to harm you, whether it's people, so-called friends, family members, or situations, you don't have to stand for it. You can speak God's Word to that enemy, and he will have to leave you alone for a season, but he will return.

When the enemy does leave you alone, you should be preparing yourself for the next battle by putting on the Whole Armor of God that we learn about in Ephesians 6 and by reading His Word. The enemy left Jesus alone for a season. Remember the mountain top experience? Satan tried to tempt Jesus but failed because Jesus spoke the Scriptures back to him. So, the enemy had to flee out of Jesus' presence. Another time the enemy came back in the presence of Jesus was when He was on the cross. The enemy thought the cross would be the end of Jesus once and for all, but death had no sting; the grave couldn't hold our Savior, Jesus Christ. Hallelujah! Thank You Jesus!

Time moved on, but my season of trials came again. THE OLD RAPIST moved in, and all hell broke loose. At this time, I was unaware that he was the devil that God was showing me on the wall. I ended up being raped and molested by him, but this time he was not dark and scary looking like the others. He was tall, thin, light-skinned, and with good hair, as we say.

Back in slavery time, you had to be of a particular color and stature to stay in the master's house. It's funny how there is no certain stature or stain for offenders to be welcomed into your family's house. If they look good, smile right, smell good, talk good, and appear to be financially stable, we will welcome offenders in our home quickly and in a hurry, or just because they are friends of a friend or another family member, they can come in.

Every one of the men that hurt me had been to our house many times except THE NEIGHBOR. Then THE OLD RAPIST moved in with us. On this day, there was no one else home but him and me. My mother was at work at the time, and my siblings had not got in from school yet. This is the first time he raped me. I was in the living room reading a book and he grabbed me and started tongue kissing me.

He turns me over on the floor, and he starts to grind on me, with my clothes on. His kisses made me sick to my stomach as he tried to get my underclothes down. I fought with everything I had in me, but he still molested me. When he was done, he threw money on the floor like I was for sale, as if it made everything he did okay. The molestation went on for a few years, and every time it happened, it was in the living room, which I didn't quite understand why until later on in my life. It was so he could see if anyone was coming by looking through the big picture window.

Every time it happened, he would say the Rapist Anthem called, "Don't tell nobody, they won't believe you. It's your fault, anyway. It's your word against mine. And who do you think your mom is going to believe? You or me." Well, it continued to happen, time and time again. I finally told my sister about it, and finally, I told my mom. But she didn't believe me. She said she would try to catch him for herself; of course, she never did. After that I decided to never tell my mom about my other abusers.

This one night, there was a party at the house, and he came into my room. He was drunk and feeling bold. He tried to mess with me, but my mom came in and asked him what he was doing, and he said he was telling us goodnight. That was the closest it ever came to my mom catching him. That hurt me so bad. I never understood why I always made my sister sleep between me and the closet, but now I do. So, he couldn't get next to her and bother her as he did me. I was trying to keep her from being hurt by him.

Shortly after that, our friends stopped coming by to play with because THE OLD RAPIST would pinch them on their us breasts and sexually harass them. He would laugh about it as if it was a laughing matter. He couldn't understand that it was not a joke and that someone was frightened, hurt, and uncomfortable around him.

One good thing my friends had that I didn't was they didn't have to stay and put up with it. They could go home to safety. My childhood turned out to be nothing like I'd hoped. Now I realize why I was so rebellious, running away from home all the time trying to get away from those repeated performances. I started writing poems about the incidents with THE OLD RAPIST in June 1972.

The Old Rapist Pt. 1

I really hate to stay home alone; every time I do,
I get raped by The Old Rapist.

At this time, I am only 15 years old,
he told me to be quiet so no one I told.

I am so scared to see tomorrow,
because I know the enemy will fill it with sorrow.

With his hands roaming up and down my thighs,
I hated The Old Rapist because he made me cry.

I ask myself over and over again,
what can be done to escape his hands?

With his lips on mine and his tongue in my mouth,
I tried to scream but no sound came out.

He said don't tell nobody they won't believe you,
all this time making me feel used and abused.

Like a fool who was hurting, torn and scared,
this problem I had I did not share.

Oh! Someone come and help me please,
I need you now in my time of need.
Help me! Help me! Was my favorite word,
it's like everyone's deaf because no one heard.

When I get older, I will make him pay,
for making me think I was an easy prey.

Oh God, please help me I need you now,
I don't know what to do, please show me how...

To let go and to forgive,
but I don't think I want to as long as I live.

Why did mom have to go to work,
didn't she know I was being hurt.

Later, I did go and tell what he did to me,
just like he said, she didn't believe.

The only thing that seems real to me
is to kill The Old Rapist and set myself free.

The Old Rapist Pt. 2: Yester Year

I remember the days of yester years,
when my life was full of sorrow and tears.

I remember how much I hated him,
why was this happening to me? Why Kim?

All I wanted was to be pretty and soft,
and I wanted The Old Rapist to keep his hands off.

When some of my friends stopped coming around,
I looked at him and started to frown.

Why wouldn't he leave me and my friends alone?
Because he was The Old Rapist with a heart of stone.

I hated him with a passion!
And when I got older, I would teach him a lesson!

He must learn to keep his hands to himself
or I would cut each finger off, he'd have none left.

Every time I looked at him, I got sick.
Hurry! Run away. Quick! Quick! Quick!
He told me my mom would never believe me,
just as he said, she totally disbelieved.

When I told her, she said not one word,
I could tell she didn't like what she had heard.

Now I hate him, and I hate her too.
I blamed them both for what I was going through.

I couldn't wait until I got out of school,
so I wouldn't have to be home and follow the rules.

Now here comes my daughter so pretty and young,
and if he touches her, his life would be done.

I always asked and questioned her because
she needed to know that I would always be there.

He never touched one strand of her hair,
because if he did, he'd better beware!

Now when I see him, I laugh and grin
because I know in the long run "I really win."

CHAPTER 3

Crying Out for Help

The age of 15 and 16 is when a girl needs a mother or mother-figure in her life. A mother to talk to, lean on, and trust. A mother to support her in everything she does. My mother was present in my life, but not in every aspect that I needed. I'm grateful that she clothed me and fed me, but I wish she saw the inner me. She did not know the daughter who was going through so much pain and agony. I felt like she only saw what was outside of me, while inside I was crying out for help. My biological father was nowhere in the picture. I didn't know who he was then, and I didn't learn more until I became an adult.

Let me ask you, when is the right time to tell a child who their parents are? Is there a certain age? Who gets to put a time limit and an age limit on the truth? I wish my mom would have to me before I got older and before it stopped meaning anything to me. I believed that everything was okay and the way it should be. A few times different people were coming to me saying, "This is your father, he is your father, that's him, there he goes (on a motorcycle)," and none of them were my father. Except, the motorcycle rider. Can you imagine how this makes a child feel? I will tell you! It makes a child feel unwanted, they think that it was their fault that the parent was not in their lives. It makes them believe their life is purposeless and question their identity.

It's one thing when a parent is dead or divorced, and another when they are very much alive, and my father was and still is very much alive and well. I have many questions that I often asked myself, like: if my dad was in my life, would I have gotten raped? If my dad was in my life, would I have gone through the horrible things with men that I went through? Was I looking for my father in other men who were in my life? I had a lot of what-ifs. If I had my father or a good father figure in my life, I believe I could have avoided some trauma in my own life.

I'm so glad that my other sisters and brothers didn't have to go through what I went through (not that I know of anyway) because it's a hurtful situation. Children need to know the truth when it comes to family. They need to know the truth even if they were adopted. You must sit your children down and tell it, right now! Don't wait! Don't put off for tomorrow what you can do today! You will be glad you did because it's a weight off your shoulders and mentally puts your children in a better place. They will love you for it in the long run.

I blamed my mom for many of the things that happened to me when I was younger. I felt like I couldn't go to her for anything, and I figured she would make me handle things for myself. That's what I did anyway. I did not understand why she didn't believe me when I first told her about the Old Rapist or why she couldn't see that I was hurting. I felt I was the last thing on her mind.

I do realize that I had five other siblings she had to attend to also. But I wished she would have cared for me in a better way. If only she had watched more closely, it could have spared me some heartache. I know that being the oldest of several children, parents don't think they need much attention as the younger ones do, but I beg to differ. Look at me and my situation. Most parents think the oldest child should understand and set an example for the next child coming after. Yet, that's not always the way it should be or can be. Maybe in a perfect world, it could work, but this world has been far from ideal for as long as I can remember.

So, what was a teenager to do, where could I go, and who could I talk to? It seemed as if there was no one there for me. It seemed as if I was all alone with my hurt and pain. Will this ever be alright? Will I make it through this? As you can see, I did make it through but not on my initiative. God brought me through this, and I thank God for His saving grace. I know I could not have made it without Him; no way was that possible.

I still remember the feelings I had when I was going through my wilderness experience—all the events' gory details. Let me tell you, it was nothing nice for a child to go through. Writing this book has brought everything back into perspective. So, if you are going through some things right now, you must tell somebody. First, tell God, and He will send someone your way to help lift you out of your dilemma. When I tell you, I blamed my mom for every bad thing that happened to me; it is the truth.

OLETHA

Oh, Oletha, where are you—
I know you're busy with so much to do.

I've cried and cried so many tears,
and they're still falling after all these years.

Why weren't you there when I needed you most?
Oh, I remember you were the party host.

Oletha, I've been through so much pain;
my heart is broken, and my childhood stained.

I feel like my heart had been walked all over,
and you were around but hardly sober.

You left me alone to defend myself.
Mom, I needed you—there was no one else.

Oletha, I feel you were definitely wrong
by leaving me home alone.

He touched me, kissed me, and made me feel bad.
There was no one there for me—I was all I had.
But it's okay. Mom, I'll make do,
without your love and support to help me through.

It's been a long and rough childhood for me,
but one of these days, I hope to be set free.

Signed, 16 Year old Me

I was a pothead getting high on marijuana from sunup to sundown. I began to skip school with other friends every chance I got. My girlfriend would sign our mother's signature for us to be dismissed from school. Boy, she was good. She knew how to write every parent's signature down to a tee. I would run away from home to forget all my wilderness experiences and get away from my THE OLD RAPIST.

I started to get weary and frustrated. I was never satisfied with anything I did, I was not too fond of school, I hated most of the teachers, and I didn't like most of my classmates. But I did have certain ones I tolerated. I kept wishing that I were out of school, out of my mom's house. I just wanted to be on my own. I stayed in trouble. I became very rebellious, inconsiderate, selfish, and hardheaded because the effects of my trauma surfaced unbeknownst to me.

I was crying out for help and didn't know it. I would sneak out the window to be with my so-called boyfriend at the time. If windows could talk, I would be in some serious trouble, but my sister took the place of a window. She made sure I got caught or got in trouble because she would talk; she was going to tell it. It seemed like every time I dealt with my sister, I got into trouble. She was supposed to let me back in the window, but on this one night, my mom caught me and beat me with an iron skillet as I came in the back door.

Sometimes I think my sister had it planned for me to get caught so Oletha would keep the focus on me and off her. I must admit I was a different kind of child; I was more of a follower. Since that time, I've learned that my sister got me into a lot of trouble. Everything she suggested for me to do, I did it, but I couldn't blame her for every incident that happened to me. I am sure that the enemy wants me to blame her for all things, but I couldn't do that.

You know God works in mysterious ways because this same sister, is the one who started praying for me and tried to keep me from being a thief. You better believe I wasn't trying to listen to a thing she said because I was still living in the past. I was stuck on who she once was and not the new and improved sister.

God had changed her. She was going to church and reading Word of God but I was blind to the changes in her life. I was doing my own thing—no more church or reading the Bible for me. I was onto "bigger and better things," THE DEVIL'S DOCTRINE. This doctrine gave me opportunities to do what I wanted to do, and it seemed alright, but I was all wrong.

As I look back over my life, I know now that I was tough to handle and hard to deal with. I was crying out for help. I believe some of it was because of past hurts, and some of it was because I was simply wrong. I had to pay the consequences of being disobedient to my mom and other things I did in the past. The Bible says in the book of Ephesians 6:2 to, *"Honor your father and mother…"* This truth is a principle, and principles will work if you work them. It's a commandment with a promise so you may have a long, prosperous life. If we do not obey our parents, we shorten our days. We must understand that our parents are making us do the right things to the best of their ability. If the Spirit of God is leading them to teach us the right things, then it will be correct, and it will be the best teaching we can ever get. A parent can only teach you what they've been taught.

The Bible says in Proverbs 22:6 to train up a child in the way they should go, and if they stray from the word of God, they will come back to it. My mom trained us to go to church, choir practice, and even to vacation Bible school. When I got older I strayed from it, but I thank God that I came back to the church. I did go back to the Bible, I did come back to choir practice, and I returned to God.

The Bible also says that we reap what we sow, and I have planted some bad seeds in my life. Not all of them were voluntary. Some seeds were sown into me by force, and someone else came along and watered them. The fruit of those seeds grew out of hand; I call it witchcraft. I needed pruning, cultivating, and replanting. I was just a tare among the wheat. I wanted to be wheat, but it wasn't my time yet.

We must understand in our mental intellect that not everybody is raised in the ways of the Lord. So, there will be mistakes made and consequences to pay. Even if we are taught the Lord's way, we still go through hell. Yet if we are following the enemy's steps (Satan), we not only go through hell, but we go to hell for all eternity. I don't particularly appreciate going through hell, but it's better to go through hell than to go to hell. I realize that if I'm going through hell, I'm not going to stay in hell.

Sometimes you must go through to get to Jesus! Remember this one thing, just because you're going through something, doesn't mean you have to stay in it. Troubles don't always last. Joy does come in the morning. When we are young, our parents, or whoever oversees us, are supposed to know what is best for us, and they should be an example for us to live by. If they are good parents, we have nothing to worry about when it comes to obeying them. Often, we suffer because of our parents' sins and mistakes, and our own as well. Sometimes we suffer because of a sin from generations prior to us. Sometimes, we suffer because of our lack of knowledge. I realize now that my children will suffer for some of my past mistakes/sins and their own, and their children will suffer because of mistakes they have made, and their children's children will suffer for their parents' mistakes. It goes on and on. It seems like a generational curse to me.

Don't forget it all started in the Garden of Eden when Eve sinned against God, so we have to pay for the sin she committed. I wish I could turn back the time and know what I know now because I would've done things differently. I'm wiser now. I have more understanding of life, and I have a lot more knowledge. If I knew then what I know now, I think me, and my children's lives would be even better today. I know I can't change the past, but I can start right here and create a better future. I have learned to be more obedient to my mom now than I did back in the day. In the same way we are obedient to our physical parents; we must obey our spiritual parents—God the Father, and our pastors because they help guide us in the right way as they too are led by the Holy Spirit.

Obeying our spiritual parents are important, especially if they hear from God and are God's disciples. God knows what's best for us. We must know that we are in the right church and under the right pastor because there are false preachers, teachers, evangelists, prophets, prophetess, and apostles in the world today. Not everybody who says, "Lord! Lord!" are real followers of God. Some of them are sent from hell. They are hell-bound, taking some of you with them. It tells us this in Matthew 24:24 and the whole chapter of 2 Peter; feel free to read it.

In all His infinite wisdom, God is the only one who can send us to heaven or hell. There is no one else who has the power to do that. NOBODY! Still, we must be qualified to go to either place. All and all, God is in control of our destiny. He is the reason we live, and He is why we die. God has the set time for us to be here on this earth. When that time is up, we must depart, and no one can stop it.

We must remember that this earth is not our home. Our home is either in heaven or in hell. Where is your home? Is it heaven or hell? John 9:4 says: *"As long as it is day, we must do the works of him who sent me. Night is coming, when no one can work."* Even though it's still day for some of us, we are not trying to go out and save souls. We are too busy worrying about ourselves and doing our own thing. Many of those who were out evangelizing for Christ and saving souls, their nighttime has come and gone and are now dead and can't work anymore. While it is still day for those still living, we must be about our Father's business and do His will.

CHAPTER 4

A Way of Escape

When I think back and recall some of the things I went through in life, I realize that Satan controlled many of the things I experienced and steps I had taken. The enemy tried so hard to steal, kill, and destroy me. The enemy had no love for me at all. He wants to do everything in his power to stop you and me. He knew I would serve the Lord; he knew I was heaven-bound to the place he is no longer welcomed. Satan knows his time is short here on earth and wants to take as many people as possible to the Abyss with him.

We were made from dirt, given authority over him, and dominion over everything on this earth, and he hates it. The enemy knows we are called even when we are working for him in the world. God did not call us after salvation. He called us before redemption. We were appointed before we were in our mother's womb. So, the enemy comes to put a stop in our tracks before we could even get to that point. The devil is mad because he can't do what he wants to do without God's permission. Thank God for that because we all would be dead or on our death bed right about now.

I was still 16 years old when A FAMILY FRENEMY attempted to rape me. He thought he was all that and a bag of chips. I couldn't stand him! I like a dip with my chips, and if there was none, the chips were no good to me. Just like chips without dip, he was no good either. Even though I was a late bloomer, my body was shaped like a full-grown woman. Perhaps, my body matured faster due to the things that happened to me growing up.

My sister and I would go to our friend's parties all the time, and we would have a good time. Mom was keeping better tabs on us too. Every time we would leave to go to a party, my mom would call our friend's mom and tell her we were on our way. Once we got there, her mom would call my mom and let her know we had arrived.

When the parties were over, I would see her mom call our mom and let her know that we were on our way back home. It only took 10-15 minutes for us to get home when walking. On one particular night, my sister didn't go with me to the party. I had an uneasy feeling about this night. It was an eerie, dark, and quiet night, but I couldn't put my finger on it at the time. Afterward, her mom suggested that the FAMILY FRENEMY drive me home. Her intentions were good because she didn't want me to walk home alone. But the FAMILY FRENEMY was wrong. I believe she even called my mom to let her know I was on my way because that was the routine. I got in the back seat of the car because of a feeling I had. He drove, stopped, and that's when it happened.

I was so close to home but yet so far. It was right across the street from my mom's house. It happened all of a sudden. Out of nowhere, he rushed from the front seat of the car to the back seat. Like an animal after his prey, he was all over me, rubbing me and kissing me all over my body. Once again, I had to hear the Rapist Anthem, "Don't tell nobody," THEY WON'T BELIEVE YOU." His secret was safe with me, and nobody would believe me anyway, right? I was tense because it caught me off guard. There I was, trembling with fear, fighting for my life. I was determined that this person would not get me THIS TIME so easily.

He was going to have to fight for what he wanted, and the fight was on. We fought and wrestled, then finally I kneed him in his private area, and he rose off me quickly. Thank God, my knees gave me a means of escape. I know now that there was a God. I got the help and strength that I needed that night. God was my help, but at that time, I didn't realize it was God helping me.

I often wondered why my mom didn't check on me or worry about me or come to the door and look out to see where I was. She could have, but I don't know if she did or not. I don't know if my mom would have even seen me, but did she even try? She didn't even ask me why I was late. But I forgot she trusted THE FAMILY FRENEMY. Now that's what too much trust in people can do for you. It's always someone you least expect who brings you the most harm. You'd expect a stranger to do something like this, but never a so-called friend, and that's where we make our mistake.

He was another devil in disguise. This situation was a secret I kept hidden until I wrote this book. I'm no longer ashamed or afraid to uncover my wounds. I have accepted my hardships for what they are. I have a new mindset, and things don't look quite the same as they used to. That's what getting delivered will do for you. I haven't forgotten, but I have forgiven. It wasn't easy to forgive, but it gave me closure and the strength to move forward. When we forgive someone of their trespasses and get closure, it brings a new beginning. This incident was the fourth that I kept hidden.

OUT OF NO WHERE

I'm 16 years old, what else can go wrong?
When out of nowhere he comes ALONG.

I like and I trusted him, a friend who was close,
but after this incident I think he's gross...

With his hands and body all over me, I begged him to stop.
PLEASE! PLEASE! PLEASE!

His hands were roaming here and there,
touching my body everywhere.

Do I deserve this, is this real?
I sure hope not—I hate how it feels.

I wish I could make this all go away,
instead it's left to haunt me, it's here to stay.

Somebody help me, I can't take no more.
It seems when it rains it definitely pours.

How long must these things keep going on?
I hope not too long, because it's definitely wrong.

One of these days I hope to be set free,
with no worries in the world, just God and me.

Oh God, where are you?
Come and help me, I feel so down.

Please God come and get me now—
because there's a lot going on in this little town.

Oh God, I'm really feeling blue because
I can't find you to help bring me through.

They say God can come out of nowhere,
but I looked for God here in Mexico
and He was not there.

I guess I'm in this all alone,
with no one to talk to, not even at home.

If God is real and has all power,
why won't He come and protect me this hour?

Please God come and take me away—
where pain, sorrow and hate can't stay.

The Bible says that God loves all the little children,
this cannot be true, because I prayed and prayed
and couldn't find You.

I need You God, so desperately.
Please come down and set me free.

As days, weeks, months, and years went by, I remembered these things no more. The memories were deep down inside, lying dormant like a lion in hiding, waiting for its prey. And then, out of nowhere, the lion pounces and swallows up its prey. During this time, I felt pounced upon and swallowed up by the ones who preyed on me. But I thank God I didn't lose my mind. They harmed my body but not my mind.

During my Junior year of high school, some friends and I walked home from a football game one night. On this day, my boyfriend could not walk me home (he was sneaking around walking somebody else). He had his best friend walk home with me. We will refer to this guy as THE BROTHER because he is the sibling of THE FAMILY FRENEMY. I'm not sure if he thought I owed him something for walking me home or not, but he was determined to get himself something, no matter the cost. If anyone owed him anything, it was my boyfriend, But he didn't see it that way.

On this Friday night, my best friend and her boyfriend were walking home with us. Slowly but surely, everyone came to their destinations. Well, my girlfriend and her boyfriend always made a pit stop on Friday nights before getting home so they could do what they do. Boy, I heard so much about the pit stop over and over again. "Kim, it's a good spot to go! No one is ever there at that time of night. If you try it, you might like it," she would always say to me. I knew that the lumber company pit stop was out of the question because I liked comfort, something soft and warm.

As my friends made their weekly stop, THE BROTHER who walked me home wanted to stop too. I said, "no way!" He pulled, and he yanked, and he pulled, and he yanked, trying to get my clothes undone. He was begging me to give him some, and I didn't have it to give. So, I ran home as fast as I could. I didn't know I could run so fast; if I had known it, I could have run track in school instead of pole vaulting!

On a different Friday night, we all started on our way home again from the game. I, my girlfriend, and THE BROTHER were last on the trail. The closer we got to my house, I felt better. Because now nothing could go wrong, no one could try and harm me. I forgot the past encounter that happened to me right across the street from my house with THE FAMILY FRENEMY.

We all stood outside of my house and talked for a little while. Then my sister went into the house for a moment and said she would be right back, but she didn't come back out. So, I headed for the door, and THE BROTHER grabbed me and kissed me. I pushed him away from me and went into the house.

Several months later, around 4:00 in the afternoon, I was coming from paying a bill at the light company for my mom. THE BROTHER saw me and yelled for me to go to his house because his sister wanted me. So, I headed for their home and told him to have her come outside. He went back in for a minute and came back out and said that she wanted me to come inside. I went inside the backdoor and waited there. Then it dawned on me that he was lying. I turned to go out of the house, and he grabbed me from behind and threw me down near the doghouse. He raped me in broad daylight. Not a soul came by; no one came out of the pool hall nearby either. I'm not sure where the dog was or whether the dog was still living or dead. I laid there, hoping someone would come out of the pool hall and save me, but they didn't. It happened to me, again.

I often wonder if THE BROTHER and THE FAMILY FRENEMY had both conspired to burden me down with more pain and agony. I often wonder if they even think about it to this day, or did they just bury it down inside as I did. I wonder if either of them knew what each other had done to me. Did they have any remorse? Or was it just natural for them to take what they wanted? Had they raped anyone else besides me? I WONDER!

It was strange seeing them every day, knowing what they had done to me. I had to pretend that everything was alright because back during this time in life, everything was "Hush! Hush!" My people kept plenty of secrets, some I know and some I don't know. I believe it's time to come out of the closet with all their hidden secrets because the longer you keep it in, the bigger it gets, and it will come back later to haunt you.

Deuteronomy 31:6 says: *"Be strong and courageous, do not be afraid or terrified because of them, for the LORD your God goes with you, he will never leave you nor forsake you."* He will be with you until the end of time. I realize now that God has always been by my side, even when it didn't seem like it. When they touched me and caused harm, they offended God. I now see that God anointed me for a time like this. To help others who have been through what I have been through and tell them about Jesus, our incredible Savior.

Prayers for these types of situations can be found in a book called *365 Days of Power* by Rick Renner. It helped me a lot.

One prayer goes like this:

"Lord, please help me have the courage to lovingly speak to those who have sinned against me. Help me know how to tell them what they did wrong and kindly ask them not to do it again. If they repent and say they are sorry, please help me forgive them for what they did and then release me completely from that grievance, never to bring it up again. Help me put that offense out of my mind forever, just as you have done so many times for me! I pray this in Jesus' name! AMEN!"

I did confront three of my offenders, The Old Rapist and Brothers 1 and 2. The Old Rapist did ask me to forgive him. He admitted to me and other family members that he did do it. On the other hand, the Brothers told me they didn't know what I was talking about and for me to get out of their face. I told them both that I forgave them and went on my way. I realize the forgiving part was not for them but for me, so I could get closure.

I knew I had closure when it didn't hurt anymore. They made me think that it was all my fault but when I forgave them, I came to the realization that it was nothing that I had done. Your value is not predicated on how people treat you. I realize that my true value is in Christ and no man on this earth could ever change that or take that away. When I forgave my offenders, I took my power back. Don't allow people to control you by keeping you bound in unforgiveness, fear, or defeat.

Even though the Brothers denied the truth, I still forgave them. I kept hearing the voice of the Holy Spirit leading me and saying, "you have to forgive them." Then when the opportunity came, I was compelled to do it. After forgiving my offenders, it felt like a huge weight was lifted off of me. Even though they didn't admit to the truth, I have peace knowing that they know, I know, and God knows what really happened. Now when I see them, I can be cordial, speak to them, laugh, talk, and just be myself around them. Being around them doesn't bother me or scare me anymore. I used to be filled with so much anger and fear... but the forgiveness that God has shown me is what gave me the strength and freedom to forgive my offenders.

Sometimes God will have you confront your offenders, and you have to be obedient and not worry. Hebrews 13:6 says: *"The Lord is my helper, I will not be afraid, what can man do to me?"* Man can kill your body but not your soul. Your soul is the only thing that matters because your body is only a shell for your soul, and the shell will return to the dirt from which it came. The soul will go back to heaven.

Experience is the best teacher, and I've had many experiences and I was taught a lot from them. What I went through was never about me; it was always about someone else. We can't help a soul if we have never been through anything. If we don't get the past hurts and pains off our minds, we can't move on; we get by day after day until finally, it explodes. Why do we feel the less anyone knows about us and our afflictions, the better off we are? I'm here to tell you that it's not true. It's a lie straight from hell.

When you don't expose the offenders who hurt you, it just makes them think it's okay to rape, kill, or harm someone else. I need for you to understand that our past afflictions do not go away; they linger. At first, our problems start the size of a mustard seed and then end up a basketball's size, causing a spiritual weight upon us that we don't see or feel. But it's there, nevertheless. It also causes us to be unstable. When I finally released all my anger, all my malice, all my frustration and hatred toward my offenders to God, it seemed as if I had lost thousands of pounds.

That's what Psalms 55:22 means when it says to cast your cares upon the Lord, and he will take care of you. He will not let the Godly slip and fall. Just like in the natural, when we are overweight, it makes us unstable, and we are not steady on our feet. A lot of weight makes it hard for our feet to carry us where we need to go. It causes a lot of pain, and it takes a lot of effort to get around. It could cause us to slip and fall. The cares of the world weigh a lot, and it burdens us down too. We don't need any extra burdens.

When we give it to God, we feel much better on the inside. God is the only One who knows how to solve all our problems, and He is always working behind the scenes to make things better. Indeed, we don't know anything without our teacher (the Holy Ghost). It is hard to make it without the Spirit of God directing our paths because everything is not easy-come-easy-go. It's painful and disturbing to think about how many people have been through a lot more than I have and they just sit there thinking everything is OKAY. IT'S NOT! Then, some haven't been through as much and need to talk to somebody about their hurts. TELL IT!

The time is here, and the time is now. Just because other people think it is okay to keep it to themselves, let them. But don't you be a coward and worry about what everyone else will say or do or what your offender will say or do. Who cares! I sure don't because it was not my fault, and it is not your fault either. They have invaded your privacy and trespassed against you. Sure, you have to forgive them, but you don't have to be in bondage behind it.

When we don't take care of our mind, body, and soul, we are in captivity, and the enemy has all the power over us. The devil has us where he wants us, but the devil can't win if we expose him for what he has done and for who he is. The victory is yours if you want it; it's all in your hands. Now you be a winner and tell the world, because the world needs to know, and you need to be delivered.

I don't care if it is your sister, brother, mother, father, cousin, a friend of a friend, or a neighbor. I don't care if it's the police, firemen, or the United States president. Please come out of your closet and TELL IT. Everything I'm telling you to do is crucial to go forward weight and burden-free. I need for you to know that I am telling you the truth, and the truth has set me free. I want you to be set free as well (read John 8:36).

CHAPTER 5

Broken Promises

Along came another man. He was tall, athletic, pigeon-toed, and had a big round, perfect afro. He was older than me but was interested in me. I was afraid to talk to him at first because I knew my mom wasn't going to have it, even if I was 17 going on 18 years old. I started dating him anyway, and eventually, my mom found out. I believe she confronted his sister or him personally; I don't quite remember. But there's one thing I do remember: she wanted him to leave me alone! His response to her was: "A man is made to ask, and a woman is made to refuse." Hearing this made my mom furious, and she demanded that I stop seeing him. But there was no way I would stop seeing him now. I was very interested in him, and I had to have him. I couldn't let him go.

I continued seeing him and started skipping school to be with him. When I would skip school with friends, he would come to get me and take me home. What I didn't know, but later found out, was that I was putting a damper on him and the game he was playing with another woman he was seeing. She was white. This upset me so much, and I wanted to beat this other girl to a pulp. Not because she was white but because she was invading my space. She was my competition, and I had to work overtime to keep this man. But my mom was on my back, trying to make me leave him alone. I couldn't. He captured me.

I began thinking of ways I could hold on to him. Things started coming to my mind, but the one thing that stuck with me was getting pregnant; this would surely keep him with me. I repeatedly tried to accomplish my goal of having a baby with him, and it didn't happen. About two years passed, and I graduated from high school by a thread.

I was still with my boyfriend. Finally, I had a relationship that lasts. It seemed like all the other relationships I had been in lasted a short period, and every one of those guys had other women besides me. That's why I ended them. I moved on to the next one. At this time, I was still with my boyfriend and working at Audrain Medical Center as a nurse aide. I worked there for a little over a year, and I started meeting new friends along the way. I became friends with this one girl at the hospital, and we started hanging out now and then. My so-called boyfriend at the time got hired at the hospital as well.

It surprised me because he didn't like to work, and he thought he didn't have to because his mom was his source. She gave him everything he wanted. He was now working, and things were going great between us. Then it finally happened. The little stick showed positive. Yay! I was pregnant. I was so excited, but not everyone felt like I did, including the baby's father.

I should've known he would be angry because he already had two sons that he wasn't taking care of, but that was not my problem. He was going to take care of this one, and if he didn't, in my mind, "child welfare" would see to it that he did. Now my new friend was excited about my pregnancy and wanted to be the Godmother to my baby. I was excited to have her be. Nine months went by and I give birth to a beautiful baby boy. He weighed 6 lbs. and 3 oz. He was the sweetest bundle of joy that I had ever seen.

My mom, sisters, brothers, friends, and others all adored him. His dad didn't want him. He didn't even believe my son was his because of his complexion. He claimed my baby belonged to a white man. I never had relations with a white man before in my life. I hadn't even slept with another man while we were together. Thankfully, his mother intervened on my behalf with pictures of my baby's father, a beautiful light-skinned boy looking like the twin to my son. He could no longer deny it. I thought for sure having his son would keep us together.

That is the next question at hand. Do you know that a child can't keep parents together? Adding a child to a relationship doesn't help if both parties are not happy about it. Time went on, and I found out I was pregnant a second time by the same man. It was only six weeks after I had my first child. Well, he was against me having another baby, and my mom was too. So, they talked me into getting an abortion, which I didn't believe in doing but had no choice.

Later I found out that my boyfriend and my baby's Godmother (my so-called girlfriend) were having an affair. What a surprise! Believe me, I was surprised and as time passed by, it all made sense to me. The lesson I learned was to keep your friends close and the enemy closer. Never turn your back away from a friend or enemy because they both are dangerous.

Beware of people in your life with the SNAKE SYNDROME. They are sneaky, and if you are not careful, they will fill you with venom. The two of them ended up moving to Detroit, and I was left alone with my bundle of joy. I now understand the power of willingly having sex before marriage. It brings the two of you closer together. It creates a covenant that is hard to break, and it changes your whole mindset toward that person.

After that connection, you think you are in love, and you can't stay away from the person; you just have to be with them regularly. You start pulling away from everybody else who meant something to you, including your friends. You don't have time to hang out with them anymore. They mean less to you because your significant other has taken over. In my case, this man was significant to me and I had hopes that what we had would last for eternity back then.

I made promises with this man by giving him my body. We'd always say something like: "We will be together forever," "I will always love you," "I will never give my love to anyone else," "I PROMISE to be true to you forever." Well, here I am, over 30 years later left with many **BROKEN PROMISES**. I gave in to my sinful nature back then, and my sin overtook me. In the heat of passion, you might say anything the other person wants to hear. Be mindful that your body is the house of the Holy Ghost. You are to be holy, righteous, and pure with your body until you are married. It is worth the wait. Having sex before marriage is not worth the weight (burden) you must carry because of sin.

CHAPTER 6

Doesn't Get Any Higher than This

I was 21 years old with my little boy, and I'd moved on in life. By this time, I had a second job as a professional dope smoker.

I was good at performing tricks with the smoke from the joint too. I could inhale and blow smoke out my nostrils, make smoke rings, and make the smoke come back to me. Every day I was learning something new about getting high. I learned to use a small metal pipe if I was getting high by myself; I used a bong filled with water when I wanted a lot of smoke for a quick high, and I even let someone blow smoke through my nostrils when I wanted an immediate rush to my head.

Having a joint on you at all times was the in-thing in the '70s, and you could buy rolling papers for cheap anywhere. When I ran out of rolling papers, I knew how to use tampon paper or make a pipe out of aluminum foil. There were so many types of marijuana in the '70s: Gong, blonde, skunk weed, and several others. It seemed like the more you smoked, the more you wanted. The more you convinced yourself that you needed it, you would start mixing stuff with your weed to get a greater high.

I would mix cocaine or put some hash oil on the rolling paper to get a greater high. There's nothing like that first experience of getting high and it was impossible to reach that same goal afterward, no matter what you tried. That's how the devil comes in and introduces you to something worse like CRACK. During these times of me getting me high, I had heartaches and problems in the back of my mind that I didn't know how to handle effectively. I convinced myself that getting high was solving my problems, but it wasn't. It was just putting a band-aid on my wounds.

When I came down from my high, the issues were still there. Don't let people or the devil deceive you into thinking that drugs help solve your problems. It only makes them worse. I know it's a trick from the enemy because I've been there time and time again. I thought I was having a funky good time and I thought these were the best years, but the truth is, I wasn't thinking straight. Listen, drugs will alter your way of thinking because it's no longer you thinking, but it's the spirit in the drug.

You must know and understand that there's something unseen in and behind everything, and these spirits, whether good or bad, cause something to happen within us. The spirits behind certain drugs come to steal, kill, and destroy us, and if we don't know the enemy's tactic, he will reel us in like a fish. Have you ever asked yourself, "Why is it that everything so bad for us feels and tastes so good to us? The taste and the feeling of something can keep us coming back for more.

We are creatures of habit and we like things a certain way, and the devil knows it, so he keeps coming the way you want it. There's nothing new under the sun. The devil knows if it doesn't taste good to us, we won't eat it, if it doesn't feel good to us, we won't try it again, if it doesn't smell right to us, we won't want it. We have to understand that everything that tastes good, feels good, and smells good to us, is not what's best for us. We have to learn to take what seems bitter to us but is good for us, with the sweet (which sometimes is something we are used to doing and seems right). When we buy drugs, we are helping to build up Satan's kingdom instead of building up God's kingdom.

Satan knows that if we continue to get high on drugs or do things that are against the very thing that God is for, then he can wreak havoc in our lives. He can cause sickness of every kind to enter our bodies, he can destroy us in our mind, and he can take away our life expectancy just because we turned our lives over to him and allowed him to do whatever he wants. We give the devil permission to come into our lives, whether we are aware of it or not. Most of the time, we are not mindful that we are giving the devil permission and power over us because we are naïve and just plain blind to the devil's traps.

It would help if you desired change in your life. You can't allow everything to remain the same because it can be fatal. You will not grow or ever learn to get wisdom, knowledge, and understanding. Instead, you put and keep yourself in bondage. It's one thing for other people to put a yoke around your neck to stop you from growing and doing what you need or are called to do by God, but it is another thing to put a yoke around your own neck.

You must remember that some people are sent to you in life, and they pray on your behalf and help lift and move you forward (they got your back). Then, on the other hand, some people are sent by the enemy. They are against you and have the assignment to try to stop you. I call them appointed offenders, and you become their prey. So, be careful who you choose to listen to, including your family and friends, because the devil will even use the people closest to you.

As time went on, I found myself in another familiar situation. My friends and I were at a pool hall partying, dancing, drinking, and getting high. We were having a good ole time when out of nowhere came this dark black man with thick, black-rimmed glasses and a magnifying glass for lenses. His eyes were so huge it seemed like he was staring at me in 3D through an X-ray. He drove this big car and sold dime bags of weed, which I bought from him regularly. This night I got in the car with him to pick up my package, not expecting the following to happen.

Out of nowhere, I heard the sound of two clicks in his vehicle. I was locked in the car and could only unlock it from his side. I think he had the child lock on because I tried to get out, but I couldn't. He drove off toward a country road in the middle of nowhere. While going, he was trying to whisper sweet nothings in my ear that I wasn't trying to hear. He even had Barry White music playing in the car. I didn't care what was playing; it was not a turn-on to me. I was trying to see how I could get away from his roaming hands all over me. Just like the other offenders, he was trespassing on me. HERE WE GO AGAIN!

Suddenly, all my past visions started coming back to me, and the fight was on again. Determined not to let this man abuse me, I put up a fight. In my mind, I had made up my mind from the last episode that I would not be easy prey for the next offenders. I was ready to kill him if I had to. We fought for a while when finally, the doors unlocked. I was set free. I guess he realized he couldn't win, so he put me out of his car in the middle of nowhere.

It was pitch black out there in the country. Boy, was I scared. I walked for what seemed like hours. Owls were hooting, and dogs were barking, strange things were going across the road in front of me, there were bushes and old tall trees with withered limbs staring at me. All kinds of thoughts were going through my mind. I was scared of snakes and any other creatures that could come upon me without me knowing it. I don't know which was worse at the moment, being raped or being eaten up by the unknown. I can genuinely say now that they both were.

Somehow, I made it back to town. This reminds me of Marvin Sapp's song, "I never could have made it without you (God). I could have lost it all, but now I see that God was there for me…" I remember being terrified that night, thinking to myself, *what had I done to make men treat me the way they did?* I almost thought it was a conspiracy, WAS IT? Did these vultures plot to do these things together? Now I know it was a conspiracy of the devil against GOD in me. Satan used these men to harm me, but it didn't work.

A couple of days went by, and I couldn't stop wondering why these types of things kept happening to me. I didn't think I was doing anything wrong to cause the men to want me. I was just myself. Eventually, I wrote another poem about this incident. I discovered that writing poems were my way of being healed (my deliverance hadn't come yet) and my way of telling my story. I hope you enjoy the following poem.

NO MORE

He tried to whisper sweet nothings in my ear,
these things I did not want to hear.

I cried and pleaded for him to take me home,
to please, please just leave me alone.

I am so tired of being taken advantage of,
I have a boyfriend now, I am in love.

He pulled and tugged and wrestled with me,
I pushed and fought to set myself free.

This has happened so many times before,
but I'm determined once again.

NO!!! Not Kim!!
Not anymore.

CHAPTER 7

Wake Up!

I was almost 23, and my little boy was 1½ years old, when I entered a relationship with a man just coming out of the military. He was easy on the eyes to look at, and he had a dry sense of humor. He was very likable. We moved in together, and I became very close to him. I loved this man, and he loved everybody. I became pregnant and had a little girl by him, who was his twin. Once again, I had a dilemma—he complained that the baby wasn't his, and his mom brought pictures to prove how much she looked like him. Every cat knows its kitten. You know the old saying, "if the cats away, the mice will play?" Well, in this case, he, the cat, was playing around, not me.

As time went on, I knew it was about time for me to find another man who would be loyal and love me for me. My little girl's father and all the women he was messing around with was too much for me to handle. It was hard for me to trust him. I did everything I knew to do to make him happy, but there was no satisfying him. He had a lush appetite that I could not fulfill.

One day I made up in my mind I would catch him in the act, and it happened. On this particular night, I was lying in bed asleep, minding my own business, when all of a sudden, something said, "WAKEUP!" So, I did. The next thing I knew, I had my clothes and shoes on; out the door I went. I was saying to myself, where am I going? I ended up knocking on my friend's door to borrow her car. Now, I'm still not sure where I was going, but I got in the car, and all of a sudden, an open vision came to me. I knew then where I was heading, and I followed the instructions to a tee.

I traveled the road until I came upon this house. I knocked on the door for about 10 minutes, but no one came to open it. So, I turned around to leave, and something said to knock again. I did. The door opened this time, and there stood this married man with some shorts on but no shirt. He was drunk and hungover. He let me in and lying on the living floor was some other man's wife he was messing around with.

I asked where my boyfriend was, and he stated that he was there but didn't know what room he was in. There were several bedrooms and other rooms in this house. The woman he was with kept trying to get his attention because he was in a drunken stupor, and she wanted him to be quiet. I just stared at her, then turned away and started walking into the other rooms. Low and behold, there was another married man and another woman (who was not his wife) lying in bed naked as well.

I continued opening doors and finding the same thing. I finally opened the door of another room, and I went inside without hesitation. There he was (my boyfriend) lying in bed with another woman. I pulled the covers off them. He woke up shocked to see me, and he jumped up and grabbed me. I knocked him down on the floor. The woman just lay there on the bed, exposed and all.

I went to attack her, but my boyfriend shielded her to keep me from fighting with her. I walked out into the kitchen to use the phone. I knew where to find the phone because I used to go to that house to visit my girlfriend before she moved out and left her husband. He was a player too. I told everyone that I was going to call the police. I got on the phone and called 911 anonymously. I said to them that a drug party was going on with marijuana and cocaine. I also told the dispatcher that there were prostitutes and pimps in the house. I asked the dispatcher to hurry up and send someone right away because I was about to kill somebody if they didn't. It was the truth because I was mad!

The dispatcher asked me for the address and my name. I gave the dispatcher the home address, but I didn't give her my name. While I was outside, everybody inside sobered up and had gotten dressed in the blink of an eye. They were grabbing the alcohol, marijuana, cocaine, and the people that were committing adultery were a nervous wreck. They begged and pleaded with me to tell the police that it was a false alarm. I wasn't going to do that, so I kept talking until someone pushed the receiver down on the landline.

The phone rings back, and it was the police. I tried to answer it, but they wouldn't let me. The adulterers were begging me not to tell their spouses either. What you do at night will come to light, as it did on this day. They should have read Hebrews 13:4 which says: *"Let marriage be held in honor among all, and let the marriage bed be undefiled, or God will judge the sexually immoral and adulterous."* A few minutes later, you could hear the sirens coming. So, I went out the door and got in the car to drive off when my boyfriend jumped on the hood of the car trying to stop me. I kept driving, and he kept holding onto the windshield wipers. Finally, they broke, and he fell off the car.

That's how our relationship ended. I went home, packed my ex's things, and took them to the other woman's house. I knocked on the door to give them to her, but she wouldn't let me in. So, I threw his clothes in her yard while yelling at the top of my lungs. Now, as I look back, I realize all that screaming and hollering I did were unnecessary. It made me look like an idiot, too, chasing down a man who didn't belong to me. We were not even engaged or married and had never talked about getting married. But there I was, acting a fool. When you are in love or lust, it will make you do some crazy things, and I did it—all in the name of love.

I am so glad the Holy Spirit woke me up and sent me on that assignment because that journey got me to where I am today.

What a process! As my journey continued, I still wasn't quite sure of myself and who I was. I questioned the reason for my existence. I knew I had a purpose I was trying to find, not knowing that I had it all along. God's will is my purpose. God knew the plan He had for me. He knew all the struggles that were ahead of me. I, on the other hand, didn't know them. I was unaware of how to seek God for what I wanted, so I sought man instead. What a terrible thing to do.

I felt like something was missing from my life if there was no man in it. I kept searching, but what I needed couldn't be found in a friend or man. I thought I had it all figured out until I met Jesus. I didn't know that I had a friend in Jesus, but I do now. I didn't know I could reach Him any time of the day or night, but I do now. I didn't know I could talk to this Jesus, and He could hear me, but I do now. When you are in the presence of God, there is such a SWEET, SWEET aroma, which is an attribute of God. Now I know that He was there for me all along. When I got to know God, I stopped making all the same mistakes.

CHAPTER 8

Shadows

I was just a shadow of the Kim God designed me to be. God knew He had to get me out of the lifestyle I was in because I wouldn't have made it. He knew I needed a get-out-of-jail free card because I was going down the wrong road fast. I thank God for using my son to take me out of my hometown, and he led me to Kansas City, Missouri, which was my green pasture. That's what a Shepherd does. He takes care of his sheep (children).

It was beautiful and full of life there. I found my calling there. I was in a land of plenty, and I had everything I needed. I still do. I couldn't complain about anything. It was my land of milk and honey. I lived by the water, and it was peaceful. I could go down by the lake and read and get plenty of understanding. I could hear from God a lot more when I was close to the water. I loved it there. Yet, I learned quickly not to get comfortable or complacent because God may relocate me to a different place.

Often, God will put you in a better place than before. He must bring you out of your old habitat into a new one. For example: If you take fish out of the water, its natural habitat, and put it on dry land, it will die because fish need water to survive. God took me out of the environment I was dying in and put me on a higher ground. In this new environment, God dried me up, gutted me out like a fish, and took the old taste of life out of my mouth so that I wouldn't have an appetite for my old nature. He resurrected me from death to life! My death was in Mexico, and my new life started in Kansas City.

Psalms 23:3 says, *"He restores my soul; he leads me in the paths of righteousness for his name's sake."* To restore means to make new, repair, supply, cure, and bring back to a former state. It means renovation and reconstruction. Our soul goes through many physical problems throughout life, so many ups and downs, turmoil and trauma. Our soul experiences pain and heartache. Then our soul learns to respond out of our emotions, and it desires things of the flesh, which are the things of the world.

We all need restoration at one time or another, some more than others. The Good Shepherd is always in the restoration business. He restored me to life again. The old me no longer existed. I was a new creature. God put the pieces of my puzzle back together and made me whole. When I put God first, He began leading me and putting me on a straight and narrow path.

God leads me daily because He knows that I may stray from that right path if He doesn't. I tried many times to stop doing wrong, but it never lasted. Have you ever tried saving yourself, and it only lasted a little while? It's because you can't do it yourself. The flesh is powerful, especially when it's been in control most of your life. You have to want to live right. You must want to be changed and led by the Good Shepherd. Only God can change you.

I was ready for a different walk. I wanted another talk, and I started to talk differently. I now talk about the goodness of the Lord in the land of the living. I am in right standing with God. I was adopted into His family, and I have a right to carry His name. My Father's name is powerful and greater than any other false god. I do my best to wear God's nature with dignity, honesty, and pride. I strive to be holy at all times and trustworthy.

As Christians, we carry the name of the Lord with us. It is the things we do in the name of Jesus that we get whipped for. Jesus' name holds a lot of weight. It carries more weight than the President, more weight than the Pope, and the punishment for using His name in vain is death and a home in hell.

By the name of Jesus, we are blessed on our life's journey. The Bible says, *"O taste and see that the Lord is good!"* I did taste, and I know Him intimately. I have a relationship with Him, and I know that He is good!

Psalms 23:4 says, *"Yea, though I walk through the valley of the shadow of death, I will fear no evil."* "Yea" means yes, you're going to walk through the low valleys of life. We don't have a choice. We won't always like the places God sends us, but we have to trust that God knows what He is doing. I'm here to say that He has never steered me wrong. I may have guided myself in some wrong places, but God has not.

Let's talk about the low valley. Unlike the green pastures we spoke about earlier, there is no peace, no richness, silence, or growth. A valley is a low, extended plain. In this particular valley, there's no river running through it. There is no green pasture, and there are no trees to shade you. There is no rest in this place. It's the valley of the shadow of death. I used to be in the shadow of death. I looked like death, and I was on my way to hell. Death is a shadow of darkness that's cast over all of us at one time or another. Let's talk about the word *shadow* a little more.

A shadow is behind you. It's in the past. Shadows follow behind you closely and watch in secret. That's what my offenders did to me. They watched and waited for the right time to attack me with hopes that no one would know. What they failed to realize is that my God sees everything. He doesn't miss a thing, and He fights my battles for me.

My offenders weren't marked or distinct, like a shadow. They were friendly and kind when many folks were around. Still, you never would have suspected them of being a dark shadow, unrecognizable, not closely marked, having a different personality when they were by themselves. They were and still may be working for the devil. If they did it to me, they would do it to others. Be aware of the SHADOWS in your life. They are continually lurking and seeking ways to devour you.

CHAPTER 9

Love & Marriage

I met a young man in the service, and he came into my life and whisked me off my feet. He wanted me to travel with him, and I did. The traveling was wonderful, but we still were not in love with one another at this time. I knew I shouldn't have married him because my best friend at the time didn't even come to my wedding, and she was his sister! Instead, she went to another engagement.

Sometimes the writing is on the wall; we just have to read the script. I knew I shouldn't have married him, but I listened to my family members and other people talk about how much he loved me and how I should marry him. Don't let anyone make up your mind for you. Seek your answers from above because God knows everything about you. He knows us better than we know ourselves.

Jeremiah 1:5 says: *"Before I formed you in your mother's womb, I knew you, and before you were born, I set you apart and consecrated you, and I ordained thee a prophet unto the nations."* Then in Jeremiah 29:11 it says, *"For I know the plan I have for you" declares the Lord, "to prosper you and not to harm to you, plans to give you hope and a future."*

As time went on, I thought I could grow to love my husband, but it didn't happen quickly. It didn't happen when I wanted it to, but it happened when I least expected it. We grew to like each other more and more. Despite our feelings for one another, I was a good wife, and I fulfilled my role as a wife to a tee. I made sure dinner was made when he got home, ran his bathwater for him, kept the house immaculate, kept the laundry caught up, and did my wifely duties in the bedroom. I tried satisfying him to the best of my ability. No one knew that we were not in love with one another. We just loved one another; there is a difference.

At first, it was hard to be in love with him because he had a strong appetite for women. I was not the only woman in his life; there were many more. I tried to hold on to our marriage, and it was hard to do. I never messed around on him with anyone else, although I had many opportunities to. At least, not until I knew it was over. We stayed married for 13 years or longer, but we were not together for more than eight years at the most. What a shame!

I ended up chasing this husband of mine all over Seattle, Washington, catching him with other women in hotels and clubs. Some were even prostitutes. My husband was not a respecter of persons either. He told me if they had boobs and a split, any woman would do. I will never forget the first time we separated, and I went back to Missouri. He kept calling and apologizing to me, asking me to come back to Seattle, and finally, I did.

Then, I had a rude awakening. My husband picked me up from the airport, but he wasn't allowed to stay home with me because he had to go back out into the army field, so I thought. We didn't even have sex before he went back out. He was in the field for two weeks, and I hadn't laid eyes on him since he picked me up from the airport.

One day I was in my apartment minding my own business when the phone rang, and it was the military hospital wanting me to come in and get checked out for venereal disease. I was livid, and I said I wasn't coming in for no test. I told them we were separated for two months before I came back to town, and he went straight into the field before we could even do anything intimately.

They called again, and I said "no" once again and slammed the phone down. In the meantime, the hospital called back demanding me to come in. Again, I said "no." So, they told me that if I didn't go in there, they would send the Military Police to get me. I told them I didn't care, I wasn't coming now, and I wasn't coming when the MP's came either. I was very bull-headed and hated demands. At this time, I am a grown woman, and nobody could tell me what to do.

About an hour later, there was a knock at the door, and it was the Military Police. They called my name out, and I didn't answer. They kept calling my name, insisting that I was in there, but I kept quiet. One of the officers told the other guy to go to the office and ask the landlord to let them in while he stood watch. Mind you, there was no back door for me to escape. After hearing the officer, I opened the door and they took me to the hospital for testing. I was mad because I knew I was clean and didn't have anything. They checked me out, and to their surprise, they found out that I didn't have anything.

At this point, I was furious. My husband had venereal disease, and I didn't know who gave it to him. I heard the nurse telling another nurse that my husband had lied about his contact. After the nurse talked to my husband again, I was then allowed to see him. I saw my husband and I asked where he got the disease from, and there was no response—just the shaking of his head, which he always did. So, I went to ask the hospital staff where he got it from, but they couldn't tell me. So, my response was: you mean to tell me that you can send the MP's after me as if I was a criminal and had done something wrong, but you can't tell me who this other person was that gave my husband VD? They said sorry, Mrs. Miller, these are just the rules and regulations of the hospital.

I wanted to know if they would find the other woman who gave it to him, and they said yes because it was mandatory. So, I told them I would wait for myself to see who this woman was, but they told me I couldn't because the MP's had to take me back home. When I got home, I called my girlfriend up to come and get me and take me back to the military base to catch this woman, but by the time we got back there, my husband was released, and the woman was gone. I went back home and packed my bags and moved back to Missouri for good this time. Not to forget, I was seven months pregnant with our son. It's me again!

Another baby was on the way. A few months later, I had my son, and I fell in love with him when I laid eyes on him. He was a big chunk of yellow, had the widest grin ever, and the prettiest brown eyes. He was a joy to my life. Once again, a child could not keep the father and me together. I was a married woman, separated, and a single parent to my children. But thank God that He helped me raise my children. I thank God for my mom, sisters, brothers, neighbors and friends that were there to help me too. It's funny how things work out. I love it when a plan comes together (Jeremiah 29:11), and God is behind it. He does give us some of the desires of our hearts.

Everyone kept trying to tell me to take my ex back and to forgive and forget. I tried to forgive, but I couldn't forget. That was hard for me to do and I was stubborn. I didn't want my husband anymore, and that was the truth. I had grounds for divorce because of the adultery he committed over and over again. Being married requires work. Both must be willing to work on it continuously.

Whenever things go wrong in a marriage, you must learn to pray about your spouse and give them to the Lord and wait on the Lord to provide you with direction on what you should do. Never try to handle your situation without God. It's easy for people to say, "find the good in someone" and "give them the benefit of the doubt" when it's not them that's going through the situation.

I tried to find the good but could not find the kind of good I needed. It seemed like the only good I found in the people who came into my life was the NO GOOD. And as far as giving them the benefit of the doubt, I did, because there was no doubt in my mind that they benefitted from me every time in many ways. I had a spiritual, physical, and mental breakdown behind these people. No one ever knew because I was good at keeping secrets and other things to myself. I was good at burying my feelings down within me that I forgot most of the time. Unless the Holy Spirit brought it back to my remembrance. Sometimes things don't stay buried long; they come out at the right time (God's timing).

I didn't have all the fruits of the spirit, no love for myself and nobody else during this time. I felt like using people as they had used me (a trick of the enemy). I had no joy, and I was filled with so much anger, unforgiveness, and hurt deep down inside. I had no peace, and I was tormented day and night by my past. I wasn't gentle because I felt on edge all the time, thinking everybody was out to get me. But I did have longsuffering. For some long years, I suffered over my wilderness experiences or, as the Saints also called them, trials and tribulations. I began to act out, and everybody wanted to know what was wrong with me. I was different than my siblings for a reason. Now, they know why.

CHAPTER 10

Warning Signs

I tell you the truth, don't stand for everything because you will fall for anything if you do. Be sure of what you are getting into when new people come into your life. Check every intersection you come across with people, look both ways and make sure there is no yield sign. Sometimes we need to pause and take a deep breath before we continue our journey. Most of us will not do that because we are anxious for a green light in life. Those yield and stop signs are placed in our lives for a reason, and they have been in existence for hundreds and hundreds of years, as far back as Moses and Abraham.

The Bible says in the book of Ecclesiastes 1:9, *"…there's nothing new under the sun."* It has always been here and will always be here to the end of time. Every person you cross paths with will not always have the green light to move forward. You may need to yield and proceed with caution. Be mindful of who comes into your space and who you allow in your life. They're going to come, but you don't have to let them come in. Pay attention to red lights! Stop and take heed to warning signs! Remember that warning comes before destruction all the time.

Because we live in a society where we like things microwave-ready, quick, fast, and in a hurry, waiting can be difficult. The enemy wants to give microwave-ready gifts. In fact, he will send trespassers your way to slow you down, sidetrack you, and keep you from having the right people who belong in your path. I call this a roadblock, or a stumbling block put in our way purposely to stop us in our tracks. We come across many bumps in the road that can indeed be hazardous to our well-being. Often, our lives are short-lived because we in such a hurry for tomorrow to come and it isn't even promised to us.

Some people, including myself, have to learn the hard way instead of taking the easy road (sometimes listening to somebody else's experiences). Most of the time, experiences are the best teachers. We want to do our own thing and end up deceived and in trouble every time. Remember, deception started in the Garden of Eden over 2,000 years ago, according to Genesis chapter 1. When the snake deceived Eve, it affected us as well. The only difference is our snakes are not the reptiles that roam on their belly. Our snakes can be a man, woman, or child, someone who we least expect, someone close to us. They can be friends, family, as well as our enemy.

If we would listen and take heed to the warnings and stop signs, we could avoid so much pain in life. You know the word IF is a small word with a powerful meaning. If I only knew then what I know now...IF! There's a famous quote that says, "Nothing happens unless God allows it." This statement is true. God does give us the desires of our hearts, but He will let us do things our way sometimes, so we can see that our way is not the right way. It may not be in God's will, but it could have been in God's permissive will.

Meaning that:

1) God's will: He has the power of determining what we do, God makes the choices for us, He decides what He will let us do or not do.

2) God's permissive will: God authorizes us, gives us the freedom to make our own choices (and mess it up). He allows us to make mistakes, and these mistakes are not prohibited.

I believe that no choice is free, we must pay for the choices we make, whether good or bad, and the payment is due upon completion. My prayer is that you learned something from my mistakes as you read this book. I pray that you will make wise choices when the opportunity presents itself so that you are blessed and paid in full for a job well done. Life is too short to be repeating horrible performances. Don't keep going around that same old mountain. Even though it looks new, it's not.

You might even attract the same type of people to your life. Oh yeah, they look different on the outside, but the inner person is the same. They have that offender mentality, they have the same characteristics, the same mindset, but they come at us differently, using a different approach. Still, it ends up with the same results. You may be wondering why you continue to draw the same type of people? I'm glad you asked. It's because you lack something on the inside that a man or woman can't fulfill.

You need the Holy Spirit to come in, cleanse you, and fill the voids in your heart. Maybe you don't believe the Holy Spirit exists? Perhaps, you haven't accepted the Lord Jesus Christ as your Savior? I'm here to tell you that He does exist, and He gives us the breath of life. Without the Holy Spirit, we will surely die. Even now, with the Holy Spirit living in some people, we are the walking dead, existing on borrowed time. If we let the Holy Spirit lead and guide us, we wouldn't make half the mistakes we make or have made. I pray that you will invite the Holy Spirit to come into your heart today.

CHAPTER 11

Becoming Brand New

As I mentioned in the previous chapter, there is nothing new under the sun. If you look back over your life, you'll notice how things still look the same. You hear the same music, cross paths with familiar people, and even see the same devil using the same tricks, plots, plans, and pressures. You've probably even tasted the same poison in new relationships that remind you of the past. Most of the time, when we want to make changes in our life, the first thing we say is: I've got to do something different, go to other places, I've got to be more careful with who I trust and give thought to who I'm in contact with; whether it's family, friends, or strangers.

These words sound good, but sometimes they start as just that, mere words. Why? Because we aren't thinking or seeing the fullness of change! We must invite the Holy Spirit to do work on our hearts and minds. For example, when you have gotten out of a bad relationship and enter into another one too quickly, you bring along heavy baggage from the old relationship. The luggage might be full of unforgiveness, strife, hate, worries, hurt, and pain. What you need before entering into a new relationship are healing, and deliverance from the wounds and soul hurts.

One of the sayings often used a lot is: Don't judge the book by its cover. Sometimes, if I don't consider it, the book's cover might be the same as another book I've read before, with the same chapters and the same ending. So, you're pretty much damned if you do or damned if you don't, huh? I mean, I've tried hard to bring about a change in my life, and the changes worked for a little while, and then another chapter of the book opens with the same old story. Nothing is fixed or changed! Can you relate?

Another saying this reminds me of is: If it's not broke, don't fix it. The problem is, some people are broken and don't even know it. Sadly, we overlook the areas of our lives that are hurting. We believe a little crack won't spread anymore or that we won't become shattered if we don't deal with people or avoid dealing with our issues ourselves.

The truth is, some of us are like cracked glass. And when others handle us roughly and without care, we break. When something breaks, it shatters into many pieces, making it hard to put back together again. It's scary that we often look at a glass so fast that we don't even notice a crack is in it. Just because the cracks aren't visible, doesn't mean we're not broken. We should tend to all the cracks in our lives, especially the ones that are hidden. You can be broken on the inside and still wear a smile on the outside.

For this reason, we need to take a good look at not only others but ourselves; Look way down in our soul, look at the complete person, and address our soul's issues. Otherwise, we will stay cracked and/or broken. A renewing of your mind, taking off the old and putting on the new nature of Christ, getting rid of the old wineskin for the new wineskin is necessary. You may be asking yourself, "What is this woman talking about? In the book of Luke 5:36, it says: *"No one tears a piece of cloth from a new cloth and uses it to patch an old garment, for then the new cloth would be ruined by the old garment and the new patch wouldn't even match the old garment."*

Let me make this plain; you can't put a church dress or hat on a prostitute and place a Bible in her hand, thinking she will change overnight. If she hasn't changed from the inside-out, if she hasn't had an encounter with Jesus, she will not change, period. She's going to continue doing what she's used to doing, along with the church clothes and the Bible in her hand. The outside may look different, but the inside is the same.

You just can't put a new cloth on an old garment; you can't put new wine in an old wineskin. It can't hold the wine. Remember the show, *The Incredible Hulk* and how when Lou Ferrigno was his old self, his old clothes fit him perfectly? This was because they belonged to him at that time. Then, when he became the Incredible Hulk, the old garments couldn't hold him.

They wouldn't fit the Hulk because he was a new person. Another example is Superman. When he was the average guy, Clark Kent, working at the newspaper office, his clothes fit him perfectly. When he became Superman, the old garments couldn't contain the new him.

Some people try to dress up on the outside and hide who they are on the inside. Again, watch for the warning signs. I'm hoping you know that the devil can dress up too! Just like Superman and The Hulk used up energy going back and forth between their two masks, it can be a lot of work to put on masks in your own life. It's easier just being the real you! You don't have to pretend to be something or someone you are not.

As Christians, our job is to tell people of the Savior (Jesus Christ) and tell them how He saved us to lead them to Christ. Let them know about the old you and how you became brand new. Be the real you and stand up and tell somebody about the real hero, Jesus Christ. He is the one who warns you before destruction comes through the Holy Spirit and Word of God. He keeps you from going around the same old mountain over and over again. He is the one who can change you from the inside out.

I thank the Lord for changing me. I couldn't have done it on my own. You can't do it on your own either because if you could, you would have changed a long time ago. I continuously pray to learn from my mistakes the first time. I don't want to be like the

Israelites and stay in the wilderness for 40 years when it should only have taken 11 days.

When you accept Jesus Christ as your Lord and Savior, that instant, things start changing. You start becoming someone new. You don't do the same things you used to do; you don't go the same places you used to go, you don't talk the way you used to speak. You can't give your life to Jesus and work for the enemy at the same time.

The Bible says in Revelation 3:15-17, *"I know your deeds that you are neither hot nor cold, so because you are lukewarm, I am about to spit you out of my mouth. You say I am rich, I have acquired wealth and do not need a thing..."* Enrich your faith and grow in spiritual maturity with the incredible Bible. You're either going to be hot for Jesus and cold for the devil or vice versa. Yes! It is still a process, but some changes should come instantly.

When we receive Jesus, He forgives our sins immediately. But when we receive the Holy Spirit in us, He will lead and guide us into all truth, which is God's Word and His promises. We can't have the Holy Spirit in us and live foul. Your temple, your body, must be clean and holy because it hosts the Holy Spirit. Be holy because He is holy! The new wine is the Holy Spirit. When you have the Holy Spirit, you become a new person in Christ. Your old nature and way of life can no longer control or consume you. With the Holy Spirit, you change your lifestyle and the way you live because you are becoming the Genesis 1:26 person, created in the image of God and His likeness. You don't just talk the talk and not walk the walk.

People will know you belong to God by the fruit you bear, how you live, and the words you speak. Remember that actions speak louder than words. When you accept Jesus, you must continue to read and meditate on the Word of God. Get into a faith-based church, listen and learn from the pastor. Be careful what you say and do because people will start watching you like a hawk—especially ones who knew you in your past. You are held accountable for the things you do and say. Like I said before, you are either for Christ, or you are for the devil.

CHAPTER 12

My Revelation

As I look back through the pages of my book, God gave me more revelation of my life, and why I had to go through the things I did. The Lord was with me while I was going through pure hell; I was never alone. Deuteronomy 2:7 says: *"The Lord your God has blessed you in all the work of your hands. He has watched over your journey through this vast wilderness. These forty years the Lord your God has been with you, and you have not lacked anything."*

Who is this Lord God? He is Yahweh, the Almighty God, the Creator, the Father, and the Good Shepherd, the Messiah. God is watching every footstep to ensure that every assignment written in our book by Him is accomplished. Every word He has spoken is being completed and will not come back to Him void.

Remember, God sees everything, and He watches over you. He never sleeps, or slumbers and He guards and protects you just like a good Shepherd should. I should have been dead and gone, but I'm still alive. I tried to overdose, but I'm still alive. I tried to drink a lot of bleach and kill myself, but I'm still alive. I had a gun drawn on me, but it didn't go off! That's why I know that there is a God. He was guiding and watching me all along, even in moments when I refused to obey and follow His voice. If you want to be disobedient and refuse to obey God, then that is your choice. What you refuse to do, He will find someone else who will.

God tells us where we're supposed to go through the ears of our mind (spiritual ears), then we see where we're supposed to go through the eye gates of our mind (spiritual eye). We then paint a picture of what we saw in our mind until we get it into the heart of our mind. Afterward, we step out toward our destination.

The key is knowing whose voice you are following. Are you able to distinguish the voices in your head? The Bible says in John 10:27, *"My sheep listen to my voice; I know them, and they follow me."* We either follow the Lord's voice because we know it, and we have a relationship with Him, or we follow Satan's voice because we know it and have a relationship with him. One of them becomes your Shepherd.

The Lord sent me on a journey of revelation through the Scriptures of Psalms 23 that I want to share with you. It says, *"The Lord is my Shepherd."* Who is this Lord? He is Yahweh, The Lord God; He is Jehovah, He is the Door, the Great I Am, all in all, He is Life. He is everything I need Him to be, and He's everything you need for him to be as well. A shepherd is one of God's attributes. He is my Leader, my Guide, Protector, Healer, and my

Deliverer. So, the Lord is my Shepherd; why? Because I know His voice and I follow Him. You follow Him when you give your life to Christ Jesus. In return, Christ gives you the fullness of life in Him.

Psalm 23 goes on to say that *"I shall not want,"* why? Because in Christ Jesus, there is an abundance of everything you need. The Bible also states in Psalm 24 that *"The earth is the Lord's and the fullness thereof…"* so there is no way we should want for anything. We may not get all our desires, but all of our needs are met.

I want the Spirit to lead and guide me; I want to be obedient to the Word of God and go where He sends me. Don't you? He (The Shepherd) makes me lie down in green pastures. It's time to get off your feet and rest in this wealthy place. The green pastures symbolize that there are life and growth. There is fertilization in the soil of these pastures.

When we look at green grass, it stands up tall; it's not wilted or barely hanging on because the still waters keep it nourished. When we are in green pastures, we are in a wealthy place; we are rich spiritually, physically, mentally, and financially. There is no sickness or disease there. But symptoms do come and go, and we have to be sound in our minds to realize that.

The word *pasture* has an S on its end in this verse, meaning that there's plenty of fields and life. A pasture has grass for grazing. It's a place to be fed. I'm talking about spiritual food as well as physical food. Remember, there's life in the Word of God.

It's our bread and our nutrition that we need to live spiritually. There's life in natural food that we eat as well.

Let's talk about grazing just a little bit. Cattle eat or graze on fields covered with grass. When you feed, take your time, savor your food, there's no rush. Some of us don't know how to enjoy and get the full flavor from our food, naturally or spiritually. When we rush to eat, we don't get to see how good it is. We need to take our time and let the food digest properly. It's the same way with the Word of God. We need to read it slowly, savor what we read, meditate on that word, then let it digest. We can't just read the Word of God like a book because we won't get the full understanding of the love story. It takes some digging, some pulling, and some studying to get the revelation of what we read.

As the 'still waters' lead us, we can rest knowing the Shepherd is with us, and all is well. The 'still water' means peace to me. This 'still water' (Holy Ghost) feeds and restores me daily. It helps me grow. This 'still water' is my peace no matter what's going on around me. The 'still water' is a peace that only God can give.

When it's quiet, you can hear from the Shepherd, you can get familiar with His voice, and then you can get direction from the Shepherd on the next step to take. The Shepherd knows what we need and when we need it. As we are taking steps on our life's journey, we must watch how we always walk because our walk and our actions are led by a voice. Again, either you are following the voice of God or Satan. Your body language will even tell on you; it will identify who you are and to whom you belong.

Regardless of the actual language you speak, your body talks. You can talk with your eyes, your smile, and your walk. You can say a lot by the way you move. You can also talk by the look on your face or with your hand gestures and leg movements. Sometimes it's not what we say verbally, but our actions speak the loudest. What do your actions say about you? Are you being fed in the right pasture? Are you growing and living by the 'still water'? Or are you merely existing?

EPILOGUE

I have concluded that there are many types of prisoners in this world. Some are incarcerated behind bars, but some walk the streets daily, imprisoned in their minds and bodies. These prisoners are murderers, thieves, child molesters, rapists, dope addicts, drug dealers, prostitutes, and the list goes on and on. They are messed up from the floor up, they have been through something in their past personally, or they have seen things in their lives that overwhelmed them.

When we are prisoners in our bodies, we don't realize all the complications we put on ourselves and others. We don't realize that we are broken inside or even shattered; there is a difference. You take a vase that has fallen, and a piece of it has broken, you can glue that piece back together with no problem. But when something shatters, it breaks into hundreds of pieces. So, we throw it away because it's too much of a pain to fix. Prisoners who are broken seem to think they can put their pieces back together again, putting God out of the equation. They don't think about calling on the name of the Lord until they have been shattered and realize that they can't get it all together and are lost and need a Savior.

I have come to understand that prisoners are much like the chaff in the wind. The chaff is the outer appearance of something. The prisoners look good on the outer surface; they look trustworthy on the outer surface; they are gorgeous, have a nice physique, pretty eyes, long curly hair, just the way you like them. But when you remove the chaff and look on the inside of that person, you see something entirely different. Inside of them are many broken and shattered pieces that they have been carrying around for years. It has become a hidden iniquity that has come back to haunt them later on in life, and we as the victims suffer from it.

These prisoners are dangerous, dysfunctional, shipwrecked, and broken. They have physical, emotional, and psychological problems and are unstable, like the wind. Much like the wind, it is unseen, and you don't know from which direction it will blow, but you can feel it. You feel it as it touches your body. These prisoners are exactly like the wind: invisible, hiding in plain sight. You don't see them or the direction they are coming from, but you realize they are there once they are all over you—trespassing against you and invading your body either with bullets, drugs, or rape.

I have also understood that the person harming you is not the person who is doing it to you, but a spirit in that person. Just like the Spirit of God (Holy Ghost) needs a body to live in, so does the nature of the devil (the hella ghost). These spirits are no respecters of persons; they will use mothers, fathers, sisters, brothers, aunts, uncles, grandpa, grandma, friends, co-workers, and cousins. They have no age limit, color, or gender. They just need a willing vessel, whether voluntarily or involuntarily. These spirits are out to kill, steal and destroy, and they are after anybody who belongs to Christ. These evil spirits bring on the spirit of hatred and the spirit of fear because now you hate that person who did it, and you're scared of them too.

The Bible says in Proverbs 22:8, *"Those who plant injustice will harvest disaster, and their reign of terror will come to an end."* Planting and harvesting also refer to sexual intercourse. A seed is planted when a woman has intercourse with a man (willingly or unwillingly), and he releases sperm into her. The seed then produces a HARVEST, whether it's a pregnancy, a transmitted disease, or even one losing their mind because of the encounter. No matter how the incident happens, just know the culprit will reap what they sow. In other words, it's saying that our circumstances and situations will not last forever. Your enemies will not be able to continue to do the same things over and over again for long. Their time is winding down and coming to an end. They will have to pay for what they did to you. I know you're asking WHEN? It's all in God's timing.

It's important to get closure after you go through certain things in life. You must learn to overcome life circumstances meant to break your heart and overtake your mind. It's nothing you can fix, but God can. He is a heart-fixer and a mind-regulator. He is our Creator and knows how to reshape, remold, and get us to where we need to be. When we don't get closure, it causes us to enter into relationships with baggage. We take something from every failed relationship into another relationship because we haven't been healed and delivered. We don't allow enough time to come and go before we are in a relationship with someone else.

When you heal, you will know because you can talk about it, and it won't have the same effect on you as before. You can then bless someone else by telling your story. The more you talk about it, the more healing and deliverance you will get. I am here to help someone else who is going through what I have been through. I know it may seem hard to talk about right now, but the more you talk about it, the easier it gets. It would be best if you told it now, don't wait, get your healing and deliverance! God knows when you are ready to come out of your situation. He knows when people need someone like you and me to talk to.

Often, we feel like we are inadequate, and we're not ready to be on display or put our business out there for the world to see. But God knows when you are ready. You just have to trust Him. God has all power in His hands to protect and cover you. You need God the Father, God the Son, and God the Holy Spirit (The Trinity) because the three work well together. It's a package deal.

You must have that intimate relationship with God and get to know the Trinity for yourself. It's a matter of life and death.

You are the only one who knows whether you want to live or die; it's all up to you. I'm blessed because I didn't have to see a doctor for my trauma. I didn't have to pay for something all over again that I had paid for in my past. I was made whole by the best doctor in the entire world, God the Father, Jesus, and the Holy Spirit. Try God for yourself, and I guarantee you will love Him as much as I do. In the Book of Psalms 34:8, it says: *"Oh taste and see that the LORD is good. Oh, the joys of those who take refuge in him."* In other words, check out God's credibility for yourselves. Begin to trust God and experience His goodness in your life forever.

Acknowledgements

With Love to My Three Children:

When I first conceived you, you were on my mind—the thoughts of how you would look stayed with me. The thoughts of whether you were getting enough nourishment on my part stayed with me because of the morning sickness I had every day until you were born. Thoughts of how you would grow up and what you would become never left me. After thinking about you every day, you found your way to my heart.

Everything I used to do before you were conceived had to stop because I needed to know in my heart that I did all I could do for you while you were in my womb. My heart told me to protect you at all costs and to the best of my ability. I did just that. Then you all were put into my hands by the hospital staff, and it was the most wonderful thing that ever happened to me. I could now hold you and lift you up and look at you with the biggest smile ever. I was well pleased with all of you. You were my precious bundles of joy.

Everything I thought about while you were in my womb could now be seen with the naked eye, and it did my heart good to see what I birthed by the grace of God. Then I carried you everywhere you needed to go in my arms. I felt like you were safe in my arms and that no harm could come to any of you. Then you worked your way down into my lap where I rocked you every now and then, or I'd put you in my lap to spank you when necessary. Then you made your way to my feet when you were being taught to walk, or you were busy running around as a child and stumbled upon my feet.

Now that the three of you are grown, you are not only my heart but in my heart for as long as I live. I love you more than life itself, and I pray that God will continue to bless you exceedingly and abundantly above anything you could ever imagine.

I would like to thank my firstborn son for dreaming dreams, having goals, and going after those dreams and goals. Thank you for allowing the Heavenly Father to help His plans for your life become a reality for you. I thank God for all the things you have accomplished and for you allowing me to be a part of it. It has truly been a roller coaster ride with all its ups and downs. What a wonderful ride it has been, though. I am so proud of you.

I want you to continue to dream and to go after those dreams. Remember, without dreams, people perish, but a dream fulfilled is a tree of life (Proverbs 13:12). Because of what God has allowed you to become, I, too, understand that my dreams can become a reality. I know that I can do all things through Christ who strengthens me (Philippians 4:13). You are truly a blessing to me. THANK YOU for being the greatest YOU – YOU can be.

I would like to thank my daughter for presenting to me the book, *Childhood Memories*, along with the diary you gave me on my birthday, in November of 2000. To be truthful, it was that book which God used to open my eyes to remember my past, so I could see where I had been until this present time. Thank you for being obedient to what God wanted me to have on this birthday. I also want to thank you and God for setting your dreams and visions in order and bringing them into manifestation. It is good to see you doing what your heart desires. God truly gives us the desires of our hearts according to His will.

You are truly an inspiration to me and a joy to have in my life. The Bible says that in the last days, He will pour His Spirit upon all people, our sons and daughters will prophesy, and they will see visions, and our old men will dream dreams (Acts 2:17). I do see God's Spirit all over you and in you. I pray that you will continue to let the Holy Spirit teach you, lead you and guide you because in doing so, you can't go wrong. Remember, if God is for you, who can be against you? There's nothing man can do to you; man can't take your soul.

Thank you for allowing me to be a part of you and my grandson's life. Continue being the best role model you can be for your son, and he will always remember what to look for in a wife when he grows up. You are a true model of a woman and a lady. Continue being the best YOU -YOU can be.

I would like to thank my youngest son for not ever giving up on his goals and dreams, even when times were hard. When it seemed as if you were not going to make it, you were and still are persistent and determined to push through your wilderness experiences into your destiny. You are loved so much. Continue to put God first in all you do, and you will see the blessings of God in the land of the living.

All God's blessings are yes and amen. You have helped me to see that we are not too young or too old to accomplish our dreams. I thank you for allowing me to be there for you spiritually and physically while you were focusing on your career. It was a dream come true to see you walk across that stage, in the midst of adversity. I thank God for you. I want you to continue to be the greatest YOU-You can be

To My Grandchildren:

My prayers are that you will grow up to be what God has called you to be and that your parents will train you up in the ways of the Lord (Proverbs 22:6). I pray that you will be obedient to all God's commandments. But the one that sticks out to me most in your young age is, *"To obey your mother and father to have a long, prosperous and fulfilling life"* (Exodus 20:12).

ACKNOWLEDGEMENTS

While you follow this one commandment, I pray you will eventually follow all 10 of God's Commandments found in the book of Exodus, 20th chapter. I want you to be all you can be in the "Army of the Lord." You may not understand what I'm talking about now, but as time and your life unfold, you will see and understand what I am telling you.

I love both of you with all my heart. The two of you are a blessing to me as well as your parents. You bring life, laughter, and much energy to these aged bones. Remember to always stay focused on what you are doing, always stay committed to what you are doing, and always know that you two can do anything you put your minds to. The last thing I want you to do is always be the best YOU-YOU can be. And then you won't have any regrets because you gave it your all. You two have great role models to look up to, that being your parents and your Uncle.

To Prophet Calvin Johnson from Oklahoma:

You gave me two prophecies in 2003 at Love Ministries Church in Kansas City, Mo., that I would be writing this book. I did not see it at the time, and I thought you were a false prophet, but I am truly sorry for the doubt I had about you. I realize now that prophecies are for the past, present, and future. Now seeing this book come to pass and my other prophecy come to pass, I must say you are the prophet God called you to be. Thank you, and I pray that God will continue to bless you.

To Pastors William and Irene Cobb of Love Ministries Church in Kansas City, MO:

I want to thank you for accepting me as your daughter in the ministry. It has truly been rewarding to serve under a Pastor and First Lady as the two of you. You not only talked the talk, but you walked the walk. You not only taught the Word, but you lived the Word. You have continued to live daily the things you preached about. You both are truly the Genesis 1:26 man and woman God was speaking of. Thank you for teaching me how to be a true disciple and how to walk in the image of God. Thank you for all the lessons learned that have made me the minister that God called me to be. Thank you for ordaining me and using me for the glory of God.

To my Friend and prayer partner in the ministry, Apostle Nancy A. ORIGINAL Cobb:

I would like to thank you for being there for me, for taking me in when the enemy drove me out of my own home. Thank you for all the Bible Studies and sleep overs we had. Thank you for being one of the best prayer partners I have ever had. I don't know what I would have done without you. I thank God for you. I pray your ministry will continue to grow and that you will continue to be one of the greatest Apostles in the world.

To my Pastor/Apostle Gary L. Young Sr. and Elect Lady Prophetess Neosha D. Young:

My father and mother in the ministry here at Power House Temple Ministries in Houston, Texas. I thank God daily for sending me to Power House Temple Ministries and the Bread House. He couldn't have sent me to a better church. I have grown tremendously and have overcome a lot of obstacles because of your deliverance ministry. You have prophesied to me several things that have come to pass, and there's one thing I do know, and that is that the two of you are truly sent from God. You were handpicked just for me for such a time as this. I know God appointed and anointed you just for me. Thank you for being so obedient to God and being led by God. Thank you for being there for me above and beyond the call of duty. I have never known Pastors like the two of you. You have truly been a blessing to me.

Because of your Deliverance Ministry that you teach, I have been able to face obstacles that would have been seemingly impossible. My spiritual growth that came from the two of you has been a roller coaster (that I always was fearful of riding), but now I've learned to ride and defeat the opposition. My spiritual growth has been a Merry Go Round (because I have been like the Israelites),

I have been around the same mountains for many years, never learning and truly understanding why my life was in such a

121

bad place, until I came to your ministry and saw myself in God's Word.

My spiritual growth has been a slide (where I am now able to hold my hands up in the air and surrender to my Heavenly Father as I slide down the corridors of life and give God praise) for all the obstacles that have come my way because they didn't break me, but they made me who I am today. Because of your encouragement and prophecies to me from God to start writing my book (confirmation from the year 2000), I have endured with this book to the end. I thank you for teaching me how to complete and how to endure all things to the end. I truly love both of you and all that you stand for. I am pleased to call you my Pastor and Elect Lady.

About the Author

Kim Lue is a 57-year-old black woman that was ordained in Kansas City, Missouri, on July 13th, 2003. She got her associate degree in biblical studies at Faith Bible College on May 8th, 2004, also in Kansas City, Missouri. She also attended GMOR school of Biblical Studies in Houston, Texas. She is a proud mother of three children who are located in Cleveland, Missouri, and Michigan. She is also a proud grandmother of two who lives in Missouri and Oklahoma. She is a part of the children's ministry at her church. She spends a lot of her time in a telephone ministry helping those who need someone to talk to confidentially and sending spiritual text messages led by the Holy Spirit.

In her spare time, she likes to travel, play board games, dominoes, cards, cook, entertain, and watch Golden Girls, Andy Griffith, Matlock, Murder She Wrote, Comedies, Lifetime, and Soap Operas.

Who am I really?

I am an open book for the whole world to read. I am in the Lamb's Book of Life that is mentioned in Psalms 139:16-18, and God is the editor, and the publisher of my book (my life). He made me page by page, line upon line, precept upon precept. Everything about me is in my book, the good, the bad, and the ugly. This is a true story that God has written about me because of everything he wrote in it. I have experienced it, or I'm experiencing it now.

I will accomplish everything that is written in my book before I leave this earth. God knew me before creation. He knew this book (me) would be raped, He knew this book (me) would be a drug addict, He knew that this book (me) would be a manizer, He knew this book (me) would be a thief, He knew this book (me) would have some children out of wedlock, He knew this book (me) would have an abortion and a miscarriage. God saw the many hurts and pains that I went through and those I gave out. God wrote everything this book (me) was going to do before He published it. God made sure He critiqued it, edited it just right, leaving nothing out.

Sure! Satan tried to stop some of the things that were written, and he tried to add some things to my book of life, but God said, "No! Not so." In my book of life, there is a straight and narrow path just for me to walk because the places I've been and the things I've experienced are for the pages of my book only. Not everybody could have made it through some of the things I went through because it would have either killed them or hurt them so badly that they would wish they were dead. Sure, I know my straight and narrow path looks easy to some of you, but I beg to differ. It was not easy for me. That's why I had to walk it, live it, abide by it.

The pages of your book are just for you to walk, to live, and abide by. I thank God He loved me in my past, and He loves me now, and He will continue to love me in my future.

Who am I really?

I am the Book of Genesis all the way through the book of Revelations, where I now can see the beginning of my life and am now heading toward the end of my life. I am a new creature in Christ, and I have now laid down my grave clothes and have picked up Righteousness. Who am I really? I AM THE CHILD OF THE MOST HIGH GOD, anointed and appointed to do His will, and then I'm going back home where I came from— HEAVEN.

My new address will be:

Kim Lue

C/O God the Father, God the Son, God the Holy Spirit

77777 Straight Street,

New Jerusalem, 88888

THE END

CPSIA information can be obtained
at www.ICGtesting.com
Printed in the USA
JSHW062321160722
28167JS00003B/231